THIS
BOOK COULD
CHANGE YOUR
LIFE!

The Art and Craft
of
SUCCESS

The Art and Craft
of
SUCCESS

10 Steps

OSTARO

Svarg Syndicate Inc.
303 5th Ave., Suite 1909
New York, N.Y. 10016

The Art and Craft of Success:
10 Steps

ISBN 0-9707196-3-9

Library of Congress Control Number
00-092714

Positive thinking leads
to positive results
—Ostaro

This book is humbly dedicated to my guru, Sri Paramahansa Yogananda, founder of Self-Realization Fellowship in the USA.

Contents

Illustrations

 # Preface

There are books that entertain us mentally, books that elevate us spiritually, books that heighten our imagination, books that have philosophical wisdom for the evolution of the soul, and books that are meant to help us succeed in the battle of life—books that are of practical utility meant for the material plane. One book cannot help us on every plane (physical, mental and spiritual). We need the help of different books at our various stages of life. The choice of the right book is vital because a wrong book can lead us astray and waste precious time.

This book was written to help you in very practical ways. By doing the right things, you will better fit within the design of creation. This book does not contain a panacea for all human problems, but it does indicate ways in which our lifestyle can be improved by avoiding common mistakes.

Time is so limited. According to the Bible, our age is three score and ten. That is not much, yet we waste more than one third in useless pursuits. How little "real time" we have!

The main subject of this book is threefold—a person, an obstacle and the goal. Every time we want to get somewhere, an obstacle or obstacles have to be overcome. When we fail to overcome our obstacles, we don't reach our goal. That is called "failure."

One example of an obstacle is making a mistake in the choice of people with whom you associate. It is my conservative guess that if you associate with even two wrong people (whose vibrations conflict with your own), your chances of success will be reduced by 70 percent. On the other hand, being with people who harmonize with you confers a great boon and helps you enormously to achieve your aims, by means of positive vibrational impact.

Another point of great importance is our developmental stage, which has a great deal to do with our maturity of mind and our energy level. Without considering these two points carefully, the total outcome of a human life can be trivial. Most people do not seem to have their goals set within any time frame. We have to decide where we want to go, and in what time frame within our developmental stage of life.

It will be an art and a craft to achieve success in the twenty-first century. Are you ready to cope with the challenges you will encounter as a result of the development of mental science—when mind, rather than bulldozers, will be the prime mover? Telepathic communication, absent healing and astral travel will be in vogue. Our problems will be more psychological than material.

The nature of the challenges we have to face will be more complex, since twentieth century technology has made life comfortable on the material plane, and very *un*comfortable on the mental and spiritual levels. So we need to get ready mentally, physically, and spiritually for the changes, which are coming quickly. The developments and changes will be brought about socially and economically because of the latest scientific research.

You are alive to see the dawn of the new age—the age of mental science is at hand. Globalization will bring about the amalgamation of various cultures of the East and West. What can we do to equip ourselves to keep pace with these technological advances and economic strides as they develop? Are we really prepared for the space age and the age of fiber optics? For a credit society represented by ATMs and a plastic economy? For a world wherein the global production of food has not kept pace with the growth in world population?

This book will help you prepare to meet the challenges of the twenty-first century socially, mentally and financially. When we don't know how to adapt—and can admit we don't know how—we can team up with others who know better; our combined efforts will help bring about universal prosperity.

Since the dawn of the Aquarian Age (precession of the Sun from Pisces to Aquarius began in the eighteenth century), there have been many changes all over the globe. There is a tilt in the axis of the earth that is causing climatic changes in the East and West—the West will become more temperate, and that will influence the vegetation. The axial tilt is causing land to appear or disappear in different parts of the globe, as waters rise or fall in response to these changes.

We—humanity as a whole—will be forced to change our thinking patterns and priorities. This applies equally to world leaders. As the age of mind begins, changing us and our world, our values must also change. This means, in practical terms, that although a leader may now be winning elections in his small community by fulfilling the material basic needs of people, future leaders will have to arrange their priorities to cater to the mental and spiritual needs of their electorate, as well as their material needs. This change must take place in the age of mind, when mental sciences will be studied with a passion, for hundreds of years to come.

What made me write this book? More than twenty years of research have convinced me that most published books cater merely to the mind, especially in the West, where intellect is preponderant. Such books, although they serve a great need, leave a void and create an imbalance between the physical, mental and spiritual planes which leads to innumerable complications, most of which are not apparent on the surface. The soul suffers for lack of profundity of thought and spiritual food. This led me to decide to write a book that will respond to that need, keeping in view the needs of body, mind and soul, and maintaining a balance among all three.

This book is aimed at three types of people—those who are highly skeptical and analytical, those who have intellectual leanings but still listen chiefly to their hearts, and those brave souls who are spiritually inclined but need some help and direction on the material plane.

Can negative thinking lead to a positive end? Is good the same thing as evil? Is it merely a matter of polarity? Is it possible that a negative event or condition may only appear so by way of polarity, and could give birth to the positive? We all need answers to these sorts of questions, and most people don't find such answers quickly. You will find some in later chapters of this book.

My observations and studies of geocosmic law have led me to believe that a large part of the earth is dominated by negative forces, within the law of duality of creation. It follows that only a minority of people think in a positive way. This places an enormous burden upon the rest, for they have to maintain a balance between positive and negative thoughts on our planet by thinking and acting positively. This argument applies mainly to leaders, whose job it is to lead in a positive direction.

Because of the shifts in focus in this new mind age, our faculty of comprehension will greatly improve as our attention shifts from fleshly cares and triumphs to mental endeavors and spiritual matters.

Included in this book are practical techniques that have worked for me, so that you can benefit from my experiments, research and labor.

You will be amply rewarded, should you put them into action. But act, you must.

Dear reader, even if I only succeed to a small degree in my aims, and this book helps you move more quickly past your obstacles and achieve more of your goals, I shall feel all the work that writing this book required has been fully justified.

—OSTARO

He writes nothing whose writings are not read.

—Martial Epigram

 # Acknowledgments

I am especially grateful to the Higher Power who gave me the ideas that form the cornerstones of the foundation upon which this book is based.

Heartfelt gratitude is due to my guru, without whose blessings this work would never be fruitful or serve any useful purpose.

My deep appreciation for Zoa D. Goele's constant help, valuable suggestions and timely advice as a true friend; Bibs McIntyre for her inestimable help, insightful suggestions and useful counsel in improving its content; and all my faithful clients and friends for their encouragement and good wishes.

How to Build a Great New Future

*My interest is in the future because I am going
to spend the rest of my life there.*
—CHARLES FRANKLIN KETTERING

Success means different things to different people. You may succeed in a material project at a certain time but fail in another area of life. It is impossible to succeed in all areas of life at the same time.

Love, wealth, health, and social recognition may be found in locations other than the place of birth. It is rare that a person finds love and wealth at the same place. He or she may find love north of the place of birth, and wealth south of the place of birth—perhaps in a foreign country. If you find your needs and desires thwarted, try a different city. A competent astrologer should be able to help you determine the appropriate city for what you desire most.

See figure 1, the plan of life. In this figure:
Is the city north or south of your place of birth? Note that big cities have greater opportunities and amenities for implementing big plans and it is easier to convince people, since cities attract people who are open to new ideas and have more resources. According to the law of averages, you have greater chances of success in big cities.

Proper timing of such a move is most essential, so that you enter in a positive cycle.

Create a team of people who vibrate with you in a positive fashion, so as to enhance your personal vibration in order to achieve your highest aims.

Figure 1
Plan of Life

Hypothetical Example
The Earth

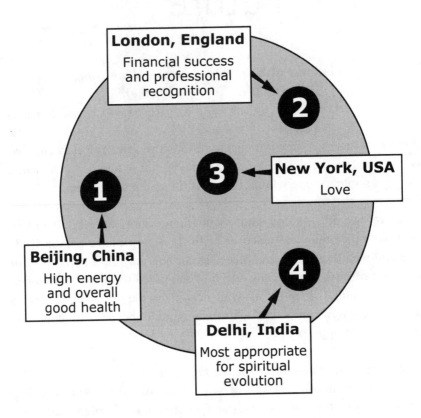

Figure 1: In the above illustration, there are different places (cities) where John (an assumed name) will find health (1), money (2), love (3), and spiritual evolution (4). Since this earth is not heaven, we don't find everything at one spot (geographic location).

Choosing the best geographical location to achieve success is a key factor. More than 60 percent of highly successful and motivated visionaries know these things by intuition. One famous example is Napoleon, who only won fame when he went away from France and not before. On the other hand, his choice of a wrong location for a battle, and bad time to conduct it, led to his ultimate defeat at Waterloo.

If the emperor had sought the advice of Pierre le Clerc (his astrologer) and heeded it, he would not have lost the battle. It is ironic that he did not choose to consult Pierre before such a decisive and historical event. He was too drunk with success to hear the words of his "lunatic" advisor, le Clerc.

Where Are You On the Path of Life?

To know this means that you must define the success you want. Before you decide what you want, you must recognize within what time frame you want it. Remember, our priorities change as we grow older. A teddy bear is very interesting to a child, but the same bear is no longer interesting when the child becomes an adult. This process continues. In adulthood, man seeks sex, wealth, name, fame, recognition, and approbation. When his energy level starts to recede with advancing age, a person becomes more and more concerned about personal health, and greater attention is paid to health matters.

Cornerstones of Success

Here is an example of the technique for achieving success. John Gordon wants to make a million dollars in real estate. His material success will depend upon three main factors:

Is John in the right place? The right geographical location is most pertinent to the project.

Is he starting at a propitious time? Choosing an appropriate time, when the circumstances will harmonize with us, will be most helpful toward the success of the project.

Does John have the right help? Each project, to be successful, requires harmonious people in its orbit; these people help make the project a success through their positive vibrational impact, as well as any work, effort or money they contribute.

Beyond these requirements, you will also need the following:
- *Persistence* till you succeed
- *Courage*
- *Expertise* and training
- *Positive thoughts*, devoid of doubts about the successful completion of your project (Root out all doubts: eliminate their causes, then eliminate them.)
- *Visualization* of the thrill of having succeeded. This helps the subconscious to bring about the requisite circumstances to help you succeed sooner and without so many hitches.

Add to this:
- Dedication to the project
- Determination
- Total channeling of all forces to focus on your objectives
- Hope and expectation as well as positive thinking (I am re-emphasizing this)
- Clear and vivid, imaginative visualization (another re-emphasis)
- Stick-to-it-iveness (and you thought persistence was enough!)

See figure 2, the molecular structure of success.

To say you know what you want and when you want it is not enough. You must be able to communicate, and convey to the subconscious mind in clear pictures, *exactly* what you want. Since the mental computer only follows our commands, any badly defined or undefined mental pictures will produce distorted messages, wasted energy and frustrating results. Garbage in, garbage out!

The proper technique of visualization that forms a most effective part of our success-producing effort has to be clearly understood. Of the five senses employed in visualization, taste, smell and touch are the most difficult. But there is an X-factor, without which the whole technique fails to produce the desired results, and that is to include, and to emphasize, your *emotional attachment* to the whole drama of visualization. Now we are at the heart of the subject.

Figure 2
Molecular Structure of Success in a Desired Project

The PTP Formula (People, Time and Place)

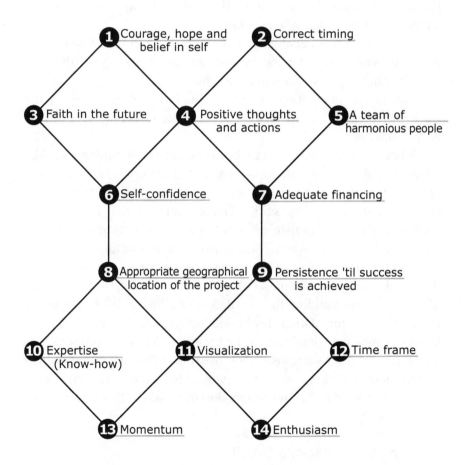

With All My Heart

We have a saying, "I love you with all my heart and soul." Without putting your heart into your project, the whole visualization process becomes merely a mechanical exercise. Heart is of vital importance; your whole being has to be involved.

"How do I involve my heart in visualization?" you ask.

Your heart represents your feelings. You must feel deeply about what you want or you will fail to get it. The project must touch your heart. Whenever you visualize the successful completion of your project, you must be moved to the point of happiness, because *happiness attracts and misery repels.*

Be careful when deciding exactly what you want. You just might get it. Are you prepared to handle success? Could you live with it? Or with the changes it would require of you?

Just as the foundation of a house underlies everything, in the same way preparation for success in a project forms the greater part of the endeavor.

When we want something to the exclusion of everything else, like a breath of air when we are drowning, it manifests more readily in the physical world. But the mould for it has to be made in the unseen. Oscar Wilde has rightly said, "The mystery of the world is the visible and not the invisible." What we see had its mould in the unseen; we know not where it came from nor its cause.

Seventy-five percent of the success of a project is in its preparation. Make your foundation solid so that it will withstand the blows of fate. It is like building the foundation of a house. When the house is finished, the foundation lies buried and you don't see it, but on it alone depends the soundness of the building. We only see the superstructure, not what supports it. No one (other than us) knows which factors contributed, no matter in what proportions, to make us a success. But we need a firm foundation to build on. See figure 3, the foundation.

Challenges—Great and Small

In life, we are constantly battling with the problem of overcoming the obstacles that stand in the way of our achieving our goals. People

Figure 3
The Foundation

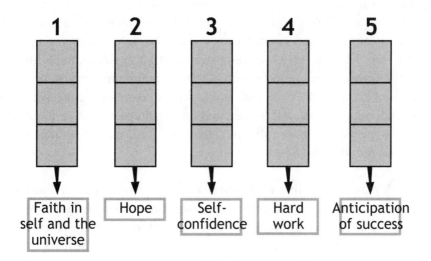

Figure 3: The pillars that support the structure of life which forms the foundation upon which we build are: faith in ourselves and the universe, hope, self-confidence, hard work and anticipation of success. One of the most vital elements is faith because when a man loses faith, he has lost the sheet anchor of his soul. So make sure you don't lose faith. The repetition of the word 'faith' indicates a great emphasis on it.

with great missions have very serious challenges posed by the hurdles standing between them and their goals, but they don't let those challenges defeat them. The chemistry of the great is totally different from that of the common herd.

The obstacles and the goal may be of various kinds, depending upon the person. For example, some obstacles may be wrong timing, a lack of opportunity, absence of people with requisite expertise or training, a lack of the right team of CEOs to make key decisions, or not having recruited enough people with the right amount of financing (for the conception, development and successful completion of the project). A wrong location could hamper the progress of the project and increase the overhead, or the failure to create a cohesive team of individuals who will be devoted and excited enough to make the entire project their own dream. The goals, too, may vary depending on the individuals. See figure 4.

A person may live on a material or spiritual plane, and success can be achieved on either of these two planes. The techniques that may be employed in order to achieve material greatness are very different from those that create success on the spiritual plane. Success in a certain field is the product of hard work, concentration of mind and determination. Napoleon, Abraham Lincoln, and George Washington are good examples of this. Howard Hughes, Aristotle Onassis and Paul Getty were also successful materially. All these men had certain outstanding qualities. Nevertheless, achieving success was not simple, even for them.

There are three ways you can learn from great achievers such as these:
• Imitate those who are successful
• Get good advice and follow it to the letter
• Do as you please, always following your own intuition.

Truly great people have a natural gift or habit of tackling any problem, no matter how small, in a masterly fashion which uses their potential to the maximum. They do the best they can at all times.

During the Russian revolution, Irving Berlin had to flee the country with his entire family. His obstacles were many. He and his

Figure 4
Man, Obstacles and the Goal

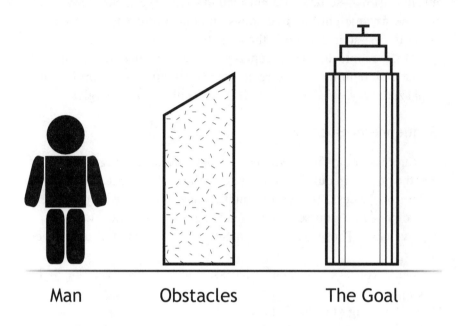

| Man | Obstacles | The Goal |

Figure 4: Our goal has to be very high to reach it, all the obstacles must be overcome. Whenever the obstacles become greater than the goal, we fail to reach our goal. Either we successfully overcome the obstacles, or we are overcome by them. The obstacles and the goal may be of various kinds, depending upon the person. For example, some obstacles may be wrong timing, a lack of opportunities for the success of a particular project, absence of people with requisite expertise or training, a lack of the right team of the CEOs, who have to make the key decisions, enough people with the right amount of financing (for the conception, development and successful completion of the project); wrong location could hamper the progress of the project and increase the overheads enormously, creation of a cohesive team of individuals who will be devoted and excited enough to make the entire project their own dream, etc. The goals may vary depending on the individuals.

family lived in a dark cellar; he was able to attend school for only two years. He wanted to write songs, but could not afford to pay for music lessons—so he could not read music. Nevertheless, in his lifetime he wrote eight hundred songs and made millions of dollars. He sold his first song for thirty-three cents.

Most people are so accepting of the idea that they will only produce something mediocre that they attempt every project in a haphazard way, without using all their faculties and energies.

Sequence of Success

Success comes in a sequence, as does failure. We ignore the fact that the people in our environment contribute, to a large extent, to our failure or success. It requires intelligence, wisdom and patience to find others like yourself and to get them to cooperate with you in achievement. Those who can't locate those others, fail at the very outset.

Once you achieve some success, you will discover that it has three parts:
- Reaching your goal successfully
- Keeping your project successful as it grows and expands
- Enjoying your hard-earned success

Achieving success by sheer luck does not guarantee you the next parts!

If you would really like to make your life a success, surround yourself with people who are successful, read books containing success stories, visit places where people are succeeding in their aims, think continuously as a successful person does, and live as though you were already a great success.

Do this until the whole thing becomes a reality to you, and you *feel* it surround you. Then you will be a rousing success, enjoying the fruits of all your labors.

Questions and Answers

Q: How can I hope for the best when no one helps me?
A: You certainly have a problem. But the trick is to *never give up*. Try to become more and more hopeful by trying and succeeding in

smaller projects. This will train you through success to acquire a greater degree of self-confidence and the courage to attempt bigger projects. Over a period of time, others will begin to notice you and offer to help, once they witness your success. Remember, all worship the rising sun.

Q: You say that one cannot succeed in all areas of life at the same time. Can I not be successful professionally and also have a wonderful relationship, while enjoying good health?

A: It is very difficult to do all that at once, because without full concentration of the body and the mind it is very hard to succeed in any given project. If our energies are not fully focused on one aim at a time, the likelihood of success is reduced considerably. To be professionally successful, one has to concentrate fully on that profession, ignoring everything else. In a relationship, there come times when everything else has to be ignored except for the relationship. The same rule applies to enjoying great health.

Q: You say people are on different stages of evolution. How can I know how evolved I am? Are there any signs that can tell you at what stage of evolution you are?

A: Most people cannot know their degree of evolution. The answer must remain as enigmatic as is the question, because the answer is only given to those who are anchored in God or have reached a certain degree of spiritual evolution. There are no easy signs that will tell you your stage of evolution.

Q: You mention that the chemistry of the great is totally different from that of ordinary people. What do you mean by chemistry, and what has the chemistry of a human being to do with greatness?

A: The physical, mental and spiritual makeup of the great is higher vibrationally than that of ordinary folks. Moreover, the great have most of their energies focused in a very limited sphere. This means that, for example, on a physical level, the great person's body chemistry operates at a higher frequency, while on the mental plane, their I.Q. and thought processes will be of a higher degree, leading to quick and clear perceptions. That makes the handling of even the most ticklish problems or nasty situations very easy for them. To be great only implies that we do great deeds, because a person is known by what he does and not by what he says.

Q: *You indicate that success and failure come in a sequence. I do not understand why that should be the case. What exactly do you mean? Does failure always follow success and vice versa?*

A: Human lives are mostly dominated by cycles that have a life of their own. During an "up" cycle a person will find it easier to succeed in any project, no matter how small the effort expended. And in a "down" cycle, one may have to spend ten times the energy to achieve the least success in the smallest project. Just as day is followed by night, in the same way an up cycle is normally followed by a down cycle, which is why success and failure so often come in sequence, though not necessarily, because the length of any cycle determines after what period of time failure has to follow success, or success follow earlier failure.

Life is short, the art long, opportunity fleeting, experience treacherous, judgment difficult.
— HIPPOCRATES, APHORISMS

Man's Unlimited Potential

The world is moving so fast these days that the man who says it can't be done is generally interrupted by someone doing it.

—ELBERT HUBBARD

The human body, as a whole, contains enormous amounts of energies of various kinds—physical, mental and spiritual. It is like a tank with a valve. We often remain ignorant of our potential and we settle for a meager existence. But we don't need to settle for less. This limitation is entirely our own fault, and it is there because of our own ignorance. We behave like elephants who are unaware of their strength. Most successful people become aware of their potential quite early in life, and learn how to release the amount of energy they need to accomplish a task effectively.

To command the energy to be released, we need the concentration of mind that these successful people always possess. Without our giving the correct command or request, the necessary energy will not be released, or it will come at the wrong time. Too early means that it is wasted, usually; too late, and it is almost surely of no avail. Or we may request less than the task will require, and thus fail to accomplish what is needed for success.

Just as the life force enters through the medulla (the "Mouth of God") at the base of the skull, so, dependent on our needs, energy is released by the body and the job is accomplished.

The attempt to use spiritual energy for material aims may be made, but it is an abuse of power. It is like using an atom bomb that costs millions of dollars to annihilate a mouse. But, of course, it is true that some of the energies can overlap, since everything—all our

• 13 •

Figure 5
Energy Reservoir

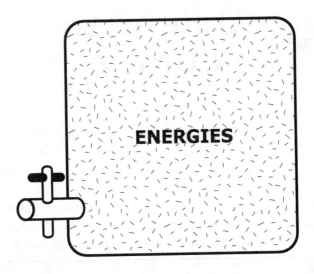

ENERGIES

Figure 5: The human body contains various energies, namely physical, mental and spiritual, which are released at different times, according to our needs and the demands made on these.

Our body is like a reservoir and has a great capacity to store tremendous amounts of energies. To store, we must concentrate mentally and fill it. When a demand is made upon any of these energies, the energy is automatically released. The amounts released will depend upon the reservoir's capacity and the degree of concentration exercised. Sports figures seem to tap into great amounts very suddenly by merely making a demand in an emergency. The tap shown in the diagram does not open unless a demand is being made from it.

Most people don't realize how much energy and which type they have in store and go through life in total or partial ignorance of their capabilities and potentialities. Thus, they compromise for a life of meager existence, even though they may have very great possibilities but not on a conscious level. If we don't know how much our bank balance is, we will not dare cash a check for a large amount. Ignorance of our capabilities is a very serious mistake. Energy is life. Moreover, being made in God's image, we can do wonders provided we make an effort hoping for the best.

forces—exist in one body. See figure 5.

To fill the reservoir of your human body with different energies:

Eat high energy foods (for low energy foods block our physical system and produce very little energy, and that only of an inferior type).

Observe mental hygiene. Thoughts of anger, greed and malice are most harmful and should be avoided.

Proper body function calls for regular exercise. Only foods that are properly digested can be transformed into energy. Undigested food residues clog the system and lead to disease. We need to leave about 30 percent of our inner space empty, not full of food, in order for the life force to flow evenly; overeating impairs our mental concentration.

To build your intellectual muscle, your mental faculties must be exercised regularly in a positive way, otherwise you cannot expect positive results.

The ideal case is to have your three energy muscles balanced. When this formula is followed, your body reservoir will be at optimum levels. Most people who are healthy, stay healthy by going on a retreat as often as needed, to a secluded place away from crowded cities. They recharge their bodies with cosmic energy in an environment that is free of materialistic vibrations, noise and air pollution. All these are highly toxic and can greatly damage the immune system.

Evaluating Your Limits

All the great feats of human endeavor are performed by making a demand for the extra energy to win. All our performance limits are self-imposed. The only limitations we have are the ones that we place upon ourselves. If you think you are defeated before the event or trial, you will surely fail, for your subconscious will bring into reality what you sincerely believe. To succeed, you must give yourself the benefit of all doubts. If you think you can, you almost certainly can. When we have a poor opinion of our potential, our doubts about our capabilities limit our thinking, so that very little energy is requested or released from the system, (in response to our opinion of our potential). When we make demands that are too small, time our demands wrongly, or make no demands at all, the result is failure. Self-doubt and fear of failure both damage our system and contribute largely to our failings. A man of doubt is no man at all. Self-doubt is most harmful.

In the Olympic games, the winners are those who know how to demand the utmost from their systems through the masterly techniques of mental concentration and self-discipline. This lets them demand—and get—the energy to break through the barriers of previous records.

When man invented the wheel, people were surprised. It changed the lives of many. Wheeled vehicles—from carts to chariots—soon were pulled by beasts of burden, from oxen to plow horses or war horses. After that, the horse carriage came along, with specially bred and trained horses that soon reduced the distance between two places. Then the steam engine appeared, using so many wheels and providing so much more horsepower. Our expectations for the future became greater. Then the airplane made its debut. We were baffled and amused, because we could literally imitate the birds and fly. These examples show how our view of the limits of human possibilities changes every time a new invention comes along, and each invention changes the limits of human potential and expectations.

Why do novelties surprise us? Our glands have been programmed for generations to limit our performance in every facet of life. All the great inventors believed in their own potential. They knew that the limits placed upon them were fallacious. So they could surpass past records—their own and those of others.

Any person can do what any other person has done. We should never say, "It can't be done."

Once upon a time, people believed the earth was flat. Until the time when the U.S. landed a man on the moon, most people thought that, too, was impossible. Why? Because we place limits upon ourselves, some from our own negative thinking, and others when we listen to our family and friends in their negativity. Keep an open mind and say, "All things are possible to one who believeth."

Patterns of Creation

To human beings, the earth looks very solid, bulky and hard. But this is only its appearance. Solid rocks, the human body, the planets, the stars, the seas—everything we can lay our eyes upon is the crystallized thought-form of God.

Everything can be rearranged, changed, moulded and improved upon. *Rearrangement of creation itself is not only possible, but has also been taking place since it all began those many billions of years ago. Indeed, creation follows a cycle and changes come eternally, without beginning or end. Since we have formed the habit of looking at life in a positive or negative way, we often conclude that things cannot or will not change, which is erroneous. Changes within creation *must* follow when the thought patterns in the mind of God change.

In the same way, humans can alter their thinking patterns by reconsidering the physical, mental and spiritual possibilities, and this creates new circumstances (that is, we rearrange the state of our thought-forms).

Growth, vibrant health, decay and death, weakness or strength, all are mere indications of a certain arrangement of circumstances, and all are subject to change without notice. Our tendencies, habits and desires can all be modified.

If you ever think you are in a rut and will never get out, you are surely wrong. Anything that has been done can be undone. Life can be changed in any manner we choose. Make a decision today to think more positively and be happy—and it shall come to pass. Have no doubt about it. No matter how different the circumstances may appear to be at times, the basic theme and the cosmic design never change in essence, since they are a part of the Divine plan.

As You Think

"As a man thinketh, so is he," says the Bible. This a deep statement, because our actions cannot be divorced from our thinking. Whatever preoccupies us mentally manifests in the outside world, forms our personality and appearance. If you are unhappy and think negative thoughts, you can be sure it will show in your face and in your posture, attitude and actions. Before you can act positively, you must think positively.

Thoughts are like bricks—not in a symbolical sense, but in a truly material way. We bring things into manifestation by positive thinking and creative visualization. Thoughts are very powerful—either in a positive or negative way. That is why we have to clean up our thinking, and set it on a positive track before we can achieve positive results. Negative thoughts create limitations. If we think and tell ourselves that we cannot lift more than fifty pounds, for example, or that we cannot learn a foreign language, or that we will always fail in mathematics, our whole system gets paralyzed, and we are ourselves are responsible for the ensuing negative results.

Before a house is built, the design is made, plans are drawn up, and the architect sees the completed structure in his mind's eye, down to the minutest detail. Only then does the actual construction work begin. In the same way, we must see ourselves as being happy and prosperous, expect good things to happen, and be confident of our ultimate success, before the conditions of our ultimate success can start to materialize.

We are each endowed with the Divine spark. Our creative potential is limitless, and we have to match that with limit-free thinking or we waste what God has given.

Thinking is destiny. We must not just accept the crumbs of fate, but improve our chances by becoming masters of our fate. No situation is so bad that it cannot be improved. Many people do not realize the power of their minds. By constantly worrying about disease and failure, they are attracting the very things they fear. Even if we are down and circumstances seem to be against us, we must keep thinking of radiant health, success and prosperity. We must keep imagining success. We must see things happening that are good, and so create them.

Make Things Happen

A person can face life's problems, provided he or she becomes aware of certain facts. Investing one's personal efforts in what we want to succeed, taking the initiative, and maintaining a persistently positive self-image can make all the difference. We should never give up, no matter how bad things look, for even the darkest cloud has a silver lining.

---

* Different, or new, circumstances may be defined as "a rearranged state of our thought forms."

To drift through life is very wrong. It is even worse to accept the way things stand today. It simply means that we have resigned ourselves to a given situation. Always bear in mind that from the very first breath of a human being, there is a constant struggle against decay and death. And that is only what happens on a cellular level!

We must train and prepare ourselves, face our difficulties boldly and overcome them. They may arise in childhood, adulthood or old age—but all can be overcome.

It is true, however, that some people never learn. There are some who are ignorant during childhood, enlightened in youth, and silly in old age, while there are some who are born fools. I firmly believe in improvement, progress and spiritual evolution, which is the sole aim of being on this earth. The wise prepare for death, but fools never think about it. Some say our whole life is a preparation for death. Maybe so. Certainly we should play our part so well today that we have no regrets tomorrow.

Very few people realize how much latent power they have within. Every person must spend at least some time every day in contact with the inner self. This brief investment of time will pay wonderful dividends in the long run. A journey within the self is quite a novel and exhilarating experience, opening up new vistas so necessary for liberation of the soul.

There are times when a very heavy price has to be paid for our principles. The greater the stakes, the greater the risk involved. We find many instances in history of leaders who never gave up and never gave in. One example is of Zulfikar Ali Bhutto, the former Prime Minister of Pakistan, who preferred to die rather than ask for clemency from President Zia ul Haq. Gandhi sacrificed his life using passive resistance to achieve justice and peace.

In July 1995, Christopher Reeve was thrown by his horse and became completely paralyzed. But he has courage, determination and optimism. The accident transformed him into a superman. He has always been driven to excel, to extend his limits, to be the best at anything he has ever attempted. So his accident has become another challenge for him to meet and surpass.

He was given only a fifty-fifty chance of surviving at all, with a break in the nerves of his spinal chord. Now, in adversity, he has had the chance to learn of his own strength. He is not only surviving, but also he is convinced he will walk again. Determination can be very powerful.

It is almost impossible to live without looking ahead. There are some who live more with the dead, mentally, than with the living, and some others who think so much about their past that they have no time to look to the future. Looking at the past can help us very much, if we are prepared to learn from our mistakes and then move forward. The advanced yogis look as far ahead as release from the body.

No matter how humble is our station in life, we must do our part to the best of our abilities. We must refrain at all times from becoming negative. Faith, hope and expectation are our allies. Be an optimist living under a clear sky. Remove the fog of misunderstanding and uncertainty by developing an iron will. Make the best use of the present. Use all existing opportunities to the maximum by doing the most you can in your desired area. Build yourself up steadily and surely, until all adversity is overcome and success attained. Keep focusing upon the object in view. Remember—time, energy and concentration must be invested in order to succeed in all things. Inaction and indifference must be eliminated.

Choose to make things happen. False expectations, which are not based on carefully sowing the seeds with well-planned actions, never bear fruit. Care must be taken to detach yourself from everything that is negative or based on a wrong foundation. Think of sunshine, success and prosperity at all times. A successful person is one who has employed all personal resources and qualities to greatest advantage, focused on the goals that are most important in his or her life-view. Go to work with what you have to create a wonderful future for yourself, realizing your dreams on the highest level possible.

Thought and action must be well-coordinated throughout the process. Dark thoughts, procrastination, lack of faith and feelings of helplessness emanate from a decadent mind. Should these symptoms manifest, take very positive steps to eliminate them by exercise of willpower within. No obstacle is too great to overcome.

"A problem and its solution are both born at the same time." It is only a question of finding the solution that already exists. There is no doubt about it. Millions of people have found solutions to their prob-

Figure 6
Taking Stock and Analysis

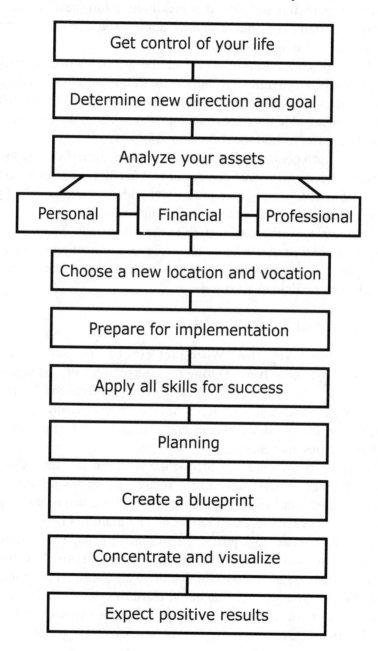

lems in the past. So can you.

The greatest test of one's faculties comes just before reaching the summit. It is on this occasion that maximum effort must be made or failure is certain. It is like climbing uphill. You can do it. A great future awaits you at the summit.

Power of concentration is one of the attributes of success. By focusing all our energies on one desired aim, we attract favorable opportunities and conditions that lead us to our goal. All great men and women are able to concentrate on one subject to the exclusion of everything else, to find the right solutions.

A dedicated person cannot be easily shaken, even if attacked from all sides. Be firm in your convictions. After deciding on a certain course of action, pursue it, no matter what others think, provided you know in your heart that what you are doing is right.

People respect those who stick to their decisions. The world lets people pass who know where they are going. Sometimes they even line up to follow-the-leader! So know your goal and keep focusing upon it with undivided attention.

Our Unlimited Potential

There is a saying that "When problems become too many, they get solved by themselves." During the course of history, as humanity has passed through different stages of evolution from the Stone Age to the Supersonic Age, our needs have been ever-changing. As we develop on the physical, mental and spiritual planes, our potential and aspirations also change.

Fifty years ago, most of us might have been satisfied with just having the basic necessities of life. Today we seek bigger and better status symbols and more creature comforts—we want more out of life. In recent years, research on the human brain has revealed many things. The human brain possesses billions of cells. The best of us, Einstein said, use less than ten percent of our brains. The British author Christian Larson has said that there are a million energies in a man; he can do anything if he could learn to use them all. If a man has a regular job that doesn't require much brainpower and has a good settled life, he is not very likely to discover his potential.

If we do not make demands on our potential, stretch its limits, and expand our reach, we never develop.

Confining circumstances, satisfaction with an existing lifestyle, or ignorance of the possibility for you to enjoy a better future and use more of your in-born personal potential can lead to a set life without any chance of real progress. There has to be strong motivation or a great desire for achievement. Great men and women, like Gandhi, Christ, Sri Yogananda, Florence Nightingale, and Mother Theresa, were motivated by a strong desire to alleviate human suffering. Their lives were spent in helping others, not worrying about themselves.

If you would like to realize your own potential, change your lifestyle. Stretch your mind, and be sure your thoughts are positive. You can do anything if you sincerely desire it. Join the company of positive people who are busy using their faculties to improve their lives and those of others.

Think your own thoughts or read good books. Go out into nature and reflect. Stretch your limits and reach for ever-higher achievement. I guarantee you will never be the same again!

Questions and Answers

Q: You say "our performance limitations are self-imposed." How do I know where my limits are without bumping into them, each time? And if I decide to raise them, how do I go about it? Finally, how can I measure my progress in this change?

A: We have two types of limitations, the ones imposed by others and the rest, which are self-imposed. We are not completely aware of what we think we cannot do because these things are mere assumptions, and they are often deeply hidden from our conscious minds. We lead lives full of contradictions and self-set limitations, that have no foundation whatsoever. From childhood, our role models (mostly our parents) impose their values upon us, and often their low expectations fix our potential limits way too low. What if our parents were alcoholics, with low self-esteem and low expectations of their own potential? This can have disastrous results upon young and vulnerable children, inculcating in them negative values that can play havoc with their lives and make them very unproductive citizens, indeed.

But we cannot put all the blame on others. We each have a free will. Let us start from this moment by taking full responsibility for all our actions. This means we have to analyze ourselves to locate our mental blocks. It is an exploratory journey. All beliefs have to be written down on paper and tested before we can accept them as convictions. Check each belief, to see whether it is based on facts or mere fiction. Discard all those that don't stand up to such a test. As humanity progresses more into the Aquarian Age, the development of mind and evolution of soul will take precedence over satsifying the physical needs and merely developing physical skills. Man shall not live by bread alone. It is very difficult to pinpoint exactly all our physical and mental limits, but it is an effort worth making, and no one else can do it for you.

If we don't know our limits we cannot hope to raise them. In a small way, by trying to accomplish relatively small things we can, in due course, become aware of our physical limits. For example, we cannot lift ten times our body weight, but we can lift forty pounds. And, slowly, we can raise that limit by two, five, or ten pounds at a time. All the limitations imposed upon us by others can be successfully raised.

Measurement of any changes in our potential limitations is quite cumbersome, but we still can have some vague idea of what we believe we cannot do. So we may make a calculated guess as to what we *can*—our inner potential. Very few of us are fully realized beings.

Q: *You said that every person must spend at least some time every day in contact with his or her inner self. Please explain what you mean.*

A: Since automation began, living in big cities has changed us dramatically. We live crammed together in big cities near industrial and other sources of pollution. We don't have enough room to move about, and we don't really have fresh air to breathe. This leads to mental tension, depression and anger. TV dinners and a couch-potato lifestyle are not good answers to our problems. All such bad living conditions impair our health.Whenever we have a concentration of people in a limited space, all those persons compete to find some breathing space where it does not exist.

Another point worth mentioning is the fact that the closer we stay to the material world, the farther we are from nature. We seem to be so much tied up in our mundane affairs that we have created a huge gulf between our inner self and the outer self, with little communication between our soul and the inner self. Such a lack of communication results in an imbalance within, that translates into many chronic diseases (both physical and mental) which are difficult to diagnose, and almost impossible to cure.

During the last fifty years or so, since the 1920s, we have begun to hear of so many conditions that were once relatively rare in the Western civilizations—AIDS, Parkinson's and Alzheimer's diseases, and various forms of cancer. Many people regard such diseases as a price we pay for our crowded, over-busy, unbalanced, "civilized" ways of life.

Meditation can create a state of harmony within, and lead you to a highly improved state of health. It is a scientific technique that produces calculable results. Meditation, practiced daily, produces health and balance. A healthy and balanced person radiates vitality and an aura of peace and tranquility. All people close to such an individual feel, and benefit from, such positive vibrations.

It is better to ride and fall, than not to ride—and crawl.

—OSTARO

Creating a Foundation

If you wish success in life, make perseverance your bosom friend,
experience your wise counselor, caution your elder
brother and hope your guardian genius.

—JOSEPH ADDISON

C hoose any three things you wish to accomplish. Set them up like this:

- A long-range goal (ten years)
- A short-range goal (five years)
- Your most urgent goal (about two years from now).

Now write down this last-listed goal in big letters as your first priority, because it is the most urgent. Mind you, any goal must be backed up by your most sincere desire to achieve it, and it must be supported by your whole-hearted efforts "to the exclusion of everything else."

The next step is creating the game plan, which requires a blueprint of what you wish to attain, described in specific detail. Make a blueprint that shows in some detail what is required, and the time limits within which you wish to accomplish all this.

Let us take Tina as an example. She wishes to buy a house within two years. Before Tina can proceed, a few realistic questions have to be answered. How much cash does she have as a down payment? How big a house is she looking for, a one-family or two-family? What kind of a house does she want? A ranch-style, a Tudor? Let's suppose she wants a ranch-style, two-family house, costing between two hundred thousand and three hundred thousand dollars.

Having established all the above, she would then go to a real estate

Figure 7
The Development Stage

Span of human life taken as 0 to 100

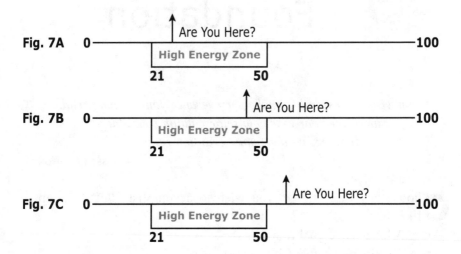

Figure 7: At any point in time, every person will be at a different stage of development and will have resources (energy, finances, time and available help, etc.) Determination of this is very important when deciding to undertake an important venture.

The stage of development where we are when we undertake a project is very important because our priorities and commitments at that stage will demand our attention and concentration of focus available.

Wishful thinking alone will not solve a pressing problem and help us complete a project successfully. Dreaming alone is not enough. When backed by personal concerted efforts, dreams transform a warrior into a conqueror.

If you are at 7A, you are in great shape because at this position you have the advantage of having a very high IQ, maximum energy level, enthusiasm, an adventurous spirit, etc. This position increases the chances of your success in any project by about 90%. However, if you are at 7B, you have somewhat more experience, knowledge, sobriety of mind and greater contacts. These factors compensate for what class 7A has. If you are at 7C, you may not have as much energy but you do have maturity of mind, resources and added experience and increased contacts, even though you may not work as hard physically but you have gathered knowledge which will be your greatest ally.

Supplemental patience is a valuable asset. It means you are careful about where you invest your money, energy and other valuable resources you may have so far at your particular stage of development.

broker and try to find out what is available in her price range. Apart from the work of finding the right property through a broker, Tina will have to supplement this effort by carefully visualizing the house she is looking for.

The technique of visualization will pass along her message to her subconscious mind, which will go to work to materialize her desire. This whole process may take a few weeks, months or years. The degree of success will depend upon what is available in the market within the price range in the community she is looking for, what kind of effort the broker is able to make on her behalf, and how well Tina is able to visualize in order to have her desire fulfilled. The time from the birth of a desire until its satisfaction is a complete process. Concentration of mind plays a very vital role in getting the things we want. Time at which we commence a project is also a very important factor. By following all the steps mentioned, Tina will have a very good chance of finding the right property within two years, a time limit she has set up for this project.

The energy zone—high, medium or low—is also of great significance and greatly influences our actions and reactions to what we encounter. Tina should look carefully at figure 7, the development stage, to find out, according to her age, into which energy zone she falls (A, B or C). All our actions and successes depend upon how much available energy we have for any new project.

It goes without saying that a person in the B-energy zone (medium, from the age of fifty to seventy) does not have the luxury of wasting efforts that will not bestow proportionate results, while a young man of twenty-two has abundant energy but may not know where to apply his forces usefully. As we become older, we begin to realize how difficult it is to recharge our bodies and use our energies wisely, so that maximum results may follow, without wasting any on vain pursuits.

There are certain important factors to be understood so that no mistakes in the process are made. What a person's capabilities are, on all the three planes, may be termed as one's *total potential*, something that is hardly ever realized because of factors beyond our control and others that result from our own failings, restrictions of society, traditions of culture, the country, and the like.

The Dilemma of Human Potential

A human being consists of many forces and potentialities. Each individual has many possibilities and limitations endowed by circumstances. A person may be likened to an automobile with a 200-horsepower engine with a top speed of 100 miles per hour. To start the car, the ignition key has to be inserted. Fail to do this, and the car will never start normally. Next, you have to turn the ignition key, start the engine, and then start to accelerate. Finally, you begin to steer, moving in the desired direction within the limits of the local driving code.

Most cars will reach their top speed of 100 miles per hour only rarely, because of speed limits imposed by the state. Likewise, if the circumstances are not favorable, even the most gifted individual may never realize his or her full potential.

The stage of development where we are when we undertake a project is very important, because our priorities and commitments at that stage will demand our attention and determine what concentration of one's total focus is available.

Wishful thinking alone will not solve a pressing problem and help us complete a project successfully. Dreaming alone is not enough. When backed by personal concerted efforts, dreams transform a warrior into a conqueror.

If you are at A, you are in great shape because at this position you have the advantages of having a very high IQ, maximum energy level, enthusiasm, an adventurous spirit, and so forth. This position increases the chances of your success in any project by about 90 percent. However, if you are at B, you have somewhat more experience, knowledge, sobriety of mind and more contacts. These factors help to compensate for what A has. If you are at C, you may not have as much energy, but you do have maturity of mind, resources, and added experience, and an increased number of contacts, even though you may not work as hard physically. But you have gathered knowledge that will be your greatest ally, and patience, another very valuable asset. You are more likely to be careful about where you invest your money, energy, and other valuable resources you may have.

It does not suffice to merely have potential. You have to do something with it. Talent alone, however great, won't achieve anything unless it's matched with other pertinent factors. The performance will depend upon the demands made by situations, and cooperation of the people in your orbit to fulfill those demands. Most people, I have found, utilize only a part of their potential because they do not find themselves in conducive circumstances; most of their faculties lie dormant because these people are not compelled by circumstances.

It is not enough just to want to do something, either. What makes us act? Let us take the case of a motorcycle. Some machines start with one kick, others need two or three. We humans are similar. Some of us need merely a hint to react to a situation, while others need to be goaded and get many kicks before they take action. Why? We say, "Different strokes for different folks."

Reaction time varies from person to person, depending upon the constitution and alertness. The degree to which our body cooperates with the mind, plus the commands given by the mind, explain the different results. When the command given is in contradiction to the highest spiritual principle, a problem will arise, and the results will be delayed or may be unsatisfactory. Those of us who are highly developed souls have no conflict between what the soul wishes—its freedom—and what we wish to attain on the material plane. Sensitive people—those composed of higher vibrations—react quickly to any change in circumstances. But if the flesh is weak, though the spirit is willing, not much will be accomplished.

Before you decide to lay any foundation, review figure 7 and see where you are.

Keep your personal affairs in order. Decide on ways to increase your financial worth. Decide on desired earnings, investments to savings and do other necessary financial planning; decide on personal aims, desires and motives.

We need education of various types to equip us to succeed in life. Academic knowledge is important, but not necessarily a must. Many people in the past have done well without it. George Bernard Shaw, a poor Irish boy, had only five years of schooling. He had to go to work as a clerk for $4.50 a month. He wanted to be a writer. He quit his $4.50 a month job and wrote for nine years, during which he made a total of $30. Yet, he became one of the most famous of all writers and made millions of dollars. He was awarded the Nobel Prize for literature.

Some of the essential qualities of those who were successful or great are:

- Reliability
- Dependability
- Punctuality
- Faithfulness
- Sincerity
- Truthfulness
- Honesty
- Continuity of purpose
- Concentration of mind on one project at a time
- Ambition
- Passion for success
- Hard work
- Cheerfulness
- Decisiveness
- Imagination
- Strong will to succeed
- Loyalty to people and aims pursued
- Persistence
- Courage
- Generosity
- Faith in the future
- Readiness to make changes
- Kindness
- Careful planning
- Friendliness
- A positive mental attitude
- Optimism
- Compassion, or sympathy for the less fortunate
- Inner joy
- Patience
- Self-discipline and focus

Sir Edmund Hillary was the first man who successfully climbed Mount Everest. To do so required unceasing zeal, enthusiasm and faith in his own strength. Without these qualities he would have failed to reach the top. Overcoming obstacles is like leaping over a big ditch. During a horse-riding competition, the one who spurs the horse and gives him a big kick when it comes time to jump over a wide ditch will overcome the hurdle with ease. Those who hesitate, end up in the ditch.

Whenever there is a problem to be surmounted, give yourself a big kick (without hesitation!) to avoid falling in the ditches of life. Remember, fortune favors the brave. Train yourself to take calculated risks first, and you will be among those who mostly win.

There is something very special about winning. The winner reaps two types of rewards: one in the form of money or a valuable object, the other as an increased sense of self-worth, which goes up a few notches every time.

Those who take the initiative have a fifty-fifty chance of succeeding in a project. Those who don't, have a zero percent chance. No one always wins. We have to battle against odds at all times, but the right kind of effort is absolutely necessary. A lazy person will never go to heaven. The concept of success without effort violates a natural law. We can only succeed in the battle of life, provided we do our part. Those who are mentally and physically lazy generally blame God for not listening to their prayers, but God helps those who help themselves.

Initiative is the spark that incites us to action. The world owes a great deal to all those explorers who took initiative and risked their lives. Without their efforts, we might still believe that the earth is flat. Enthusiasm sets the fire ablaze; only enthusiasm releases enormous amounts of energy from the human body. Invest some time and take a journey within yourself to explore the capabilities you possess. Be totally honest, without any false modesty. The results will amaze you. It is a serious mistake to believe that we are helpless beings at the mercy of some external force. Humans are the highest creation of God, and to be like a god we must first be fully human.

Most people wrongly believe that higher goals are hard to achieve— harder than lesser ones, somehow—but this is not exactly true. The process involved in raising a million dollars is almost the same as raising a hundred thousand. In fact, the larger is easier. Most rich people don't like to deal with the small fish because they have a greater understanding of money and how it is made. Their financial horizon is broader and the concept of thousands is not worth their effort. Hence, they prefer to deal in millions.

By higher goals we don't necessarily mean material wealth, either. It must be made clear that attainment of intellectual wealth requires a *dif-*

ferent type of effort. Those who are fed up with being materially poor, are anxious to acquire material riches. Similarly, those who, having been rich materially for awhile, crave peace of mind, health, and Nirvana. We tend to want what we don't have. However, we must remember that not all changes are for the better. The entire natural order on earth takes on a new dimension or shape every three months. We call them seasons. Some like this, while others resent it. Whatever you are today simply represents a stage of development that can be changed by following a certain procedure. Nature itself is impartial to the cycles and patterns that form its parts.

In order to make material progress, we must have a thorough knowledge of where we stand; we must review our specific achievements on material, intellectual and spiritual levels in the past, plus the limitations or expectations we see as we look ahead to plan our goals for the future. A person who does not bother to take stock of life has little chance of success. Take stock today and invest some energy in your own future. It is only natural to become better, and then finally the best, if we keep trying. Every defeat should be taken as a challenge, and every challenge as a test of our powers and mental prowess.

To have a goal is half the battle. A person without a goal is like a ship with no destination. The first thing to do is to become aware of what direction our life is presently taking, where we stand now, and what we plan to do in the future. You must know clearly in your mind what you want from life: your expectations. A firm determination to succeed, total devotion to your duty, and pleasure in your results will go a long way to help you realize all your goals.

To force yourself to do what you hate most, brings your negative qualities to the fore. The sages teach that we should perform all actions cheerfully. To succeed in life involves certain basic techniques, hard work and persistence. No one ever became great without plenty of hard work. It is a mistake to settle for a mediocre existence. Think of great things and sooner or later you will get into the habit of attempting big things.

Pay no attention to those who carelessly give unsound advice. Remember the saying, "God save me from my friends, for I know my enemies."

There is a tremendous degree of responsibility involved in giving advice to others. If you have a problem, the best solution will come from within yourself. For hundreds of years people have depended upon others but now, as we enter the Aquarian Age, we are learning to rely more and more on ourselves. It will take a long time to cultivate this habit but it's worth learning. A person who has not had success for a long time, remembers only his failures; choosing to remember those times in the past when you had achieved success will give a temporary boost to your ego, and may even inspire you to overcome many of your present problems successfully. The successful people are doers, not just thinkers. Create the habit of making plans and then carry them out without too much procrastination.

As we get older, we realize that life is too short to worry about trivialities. These are some of the facts I have discovered during my struggles through my own life.

Questions and Answers

Q: What helps overcome procrastination?

A: First try to do small things without delay. As humans, we change our habits only slowly. Then try more difficult things and overcome them without delay till you gain confidence. After persisting in solving problems instantly, you will start to enjoy problem-solving and become a master. When we overcome the habit of procrastination, we change our self-image and this gives self-confidence. And self-confidence helps us make a demand from our system to release greater amounts of energy to overcome any hurdle without delay.

The problem is that when we have a poor self-image, we have no track record of having solved problems instantly and consciousness of a lack of energy, even though it is in fact there in reality, blocks its release because we make no demands in the right way. You wouldn't expect to cash a check at your bank if you didn't sign and endorse it on the back. We must follow correct procedures to get right results. We have such bad habits, ingrained over generations, that our physical bodies normally operate at about 30 to 40 percent of our capacity, which leads to mediocre performance and very poor results. Or if our bodies are, or have been, sick, the mind suffers in consequence, and its capacity to judge, to discriminate, to balance right and wrong, are all impaired. Poor mental judgement leads to a sequence of failures, and we build a bad track record. Consequently, this gives us a firm belief that we are helpless failures, without hope. But this can all be changed. Do not lose hope.

Go far away from civilization and reflect upon all the problems you have without any contact with the material world. Then take mental stock of what you do have, both assets and liabilities. Clear your mind of all doubts and forget the past. Start anew with the present. Pray to the Creator for help and guidance. Go to a new town and start small. Try doing things in a small way. Keep a record of all your small achievements. Slowly you will notice that light will come, giving you increased confidence. This confidence in yourself will be made concrete by practice. Slowly try bigger and bigger challenges, until you become a master of handling difficult problems.

Caution: Remain totally disconnected and aloof from all people you know. Read no newspaper, listen to no radio, and watch no TV. This period of transition, with your self-confidence in its embryonic stage, is most crucial. Any contact with the civilized world can instantly neutralize all you have created with so much hard work.

Wait till you can control your own little environment, and carefully avoid all negative people. By following these instructions, you will have a better chance, in due course, of becoming a success-oriented human being, and reaching your goals.

Nervous people who seek instant gratification of their desires make very bad candidates for this technique. It requires you to invest patience, time, solitude, and stay at a great distance from the civilized world—plus perseverance and anticipation of eventual success.

A bad habit of procrastination created over five or ten years of violating the natural laws will take a few years to change.

Q: Why do most people fail to reach their full potential?

A: The basic problem is our ignorance of the anatomy of the human body, how it functions, why it functions, what is expected of us, what is not expected of us, why do we fail at certain times, and the rules of health and hygiene.

We normally use only the left side of the brain, rarely the right side—the creative side. We don't even know how much potential we have on any of the three planes. We live on guesses and assumptions, not knowledge. We wonder if we can do this or that, but we are not sure. Normally, we do not measure nor do we discover and measure our capabilities and limits even on the physical plane.

First we have to find out how much potential we have. I don't even know how much is 50 percent of my full potential on any plane. In ignorance, I have no chance to achieve because I have no expectations; hence, I can't direct my forces towards achieving anything.

To live a life based on the assumptions and opinions of others is seriously wrong. If your role models are full of faults, you will end up being like them. They may have been ne'er-do-wells or they may have been showing a facade. The dilemma is we usually do not question what we are presented with at our earliest, most gullible age.

The whole issue of our potential gets lost in the quagmire of our civilized culture. There are some rare souls who question everything, invest the necessary efforts to find out the facts about themselves and then re-think their own expectations. These people may have some idea of their own potential.

The shifts of Fortune test the reliability of friends.
—JULIUS CAESAR, *DE AMICITIA, XVIII*

The man of virtue makes the difficulty to be overcome his first business and success only a subsequent consideration.
—CONFUCIUS, *ANALECTS,* 6:20

Opportunities and Timing— Keys to Success

Too many people are thinking of security instead of opportunity.
They seem more afraid of life than of death.

—Francis Bacon

T here are few things more fundamental to success than choosing our timing and grasping our opportunities. Opportunities are most often created by the political climate, the economy and the stock market. Sometimes they arise from an accident, or represent a favor granted. Success is largely determined by our taking advantage of the most opportune time to find a job, sell property or buy stock. Apart from analysis, common sense and sheer gut feeling, how can we know when is the right time to make such a move?

Of course, if we work hard and keep trying, eventually we will hit a good cycle and succeed. But there are ways of maximizing the successful outcome by making an extra effort during a good cycle. The market, as we all know, moves in cycles, but they appear to be rather unpredictable by most people. Our lives, whether we are aware of it or not, also move in cycles. There are days we feel better than on others, there are weeks and months when we seem to encounter one obstacle after another, while there are months when we feel on top of the world, because things are going our way.

Opportunities represent cycles that may be favorable to success in love, money matters, health, or fulfilling a desire for world travel, to name just a few. It is possible to calculate different cycles well in advance, but to create a plan of action which uses each cycle in a positive way will involve a lot of concrete thinking, preparation and planning. Opportunity opens the door to success. However, one must be ready to act when it appears. See figure 8.

Figure 8
Reaching the Goal

Figure 8: This diagram shows obstacles marked by negatives (-). They may be a lack of opportunity, distance, bad timing, inharmonious circumstances or a lack of sufficient funds. At times, people hold us back for various personal reasons and they become obstacles to be overcome. Life seems to be a constant battle against circumstances and only those who succeed are able to win those battles while the rest are termed "failures."

The positive signs (+) indicate harmonious people who are sympathetic toward us and thus prove helpful and we can realize our dreams easily. The more positive people we have, the better it is for us, because then success will be much easier to achieve.

You will not get something without working for it. The law of nature states that you must earn the right to have something in order to get it, keep it and enjoy it. Should you not earn what you acquire, you will most likely lose it. There truly is no free lunch.

Cycles

Cycles dominate our lives. The moon has a cycle of twenty-eight days (tied exactly to women's menstruation cycle), while the sun has, approximately, a thirty-day cycle to go through one complete sign of the zodiac. It must be mentioned here that the longitude of the sun in any sign does not vary by more than one degree in a period of ten thousand years, such is the exactitude and precision of the natural law.

For centuries, the farmers of the world have sown their crops in the increase of the moon, a fourteen-day cycle. *The Farmers' Almanac* is widely used in the U.S. and is a most useful tool for making hay while the sun shines.

During a bad or negative cycle, it's twice as hard to succeed even in small things, because the vibrations around us are very negative and inharmonious. People then are very reluctant to help us materialize our dreams. In an up cycle, most people will find and invent good qualities in us that they previously never thought we had. But bad or negative cycles open up old wounds, causing us much discomfort and pain.

Human lives are largely dominated by cycles, from birth to death. When Napoleon hit a bad cycle of two weeks, he lost the battle at Waterloo against the Duke of Wellington, who was in an up cycle. In August and September of 1998, President Bill Clinton, because of a temporary bad cycle, was being shunned by his own colleagues and facing impeachment proceedings. *Cycles, The Mysterious Forces that Trigger Events,* by Edward R. Dewey, gives detailed accounts of cycles of war, famine, and stock market swings.

Opportunities can be stepping stones to success, provided they are the right ones for the person concerned. The large chunks of time when positive opportunities will occur, can be quite accurately determined well in advance by a competent astrological consultant, using the natal horoscope of a correctly recorded nativity. They will help you prepare for personal success and prosperity. There are approximately four large chunks of time which present themselves in the lifetime of an individual, when you are likely to miss great chances of success.

Opportunities may take many forms: increased cooperation from fellow workers, a promotion, chances of fulfilling a long-cherished ambition, successful termination of a long-standing dispute, a windfall of money, or a most unexpected opening for personal elevation in the social or business realm, such as a chance to become the chairman or president of a corporation—or any other hoped-for wish that may have appeared beyond reach.

A positive cycle opens doors for you, but you must then react to the breaks as they appear. You cannot expect things to fall from heaven because of the lucky cycle. Good luck, here, simply means that an opportunity exists, waiting for you to grab and use it to make things happen through your personal efforts.

It also means that you may encounter fewer difficulties while trying to succeed, as people around you will be more cooperative and friendly. They may find you more interesting, very charming, delightful, and pleasant to work with. They may discover good qualities in you that had been hidden from the gaze of most people, and expect you to perform accordingly. The spotlight will be on you because of the positive cycle.

But, no sooner has the positive cycle ended, than the same people will change their attitudes towards you and find you not so charming. The trick is to use your good opportunity to the maximum, because such chances are very hard to come by. Because of old and bad habits of reacting to things in a leisurely manner, the greatest chance may pass you by without your realizing what you have missed. Ignorance is no excuse. The penalty for laziness is the defeat of your plans, frustration, and eventual failure. Those who fail to respond to opportunities are left behind in the battle of life; they will no doubt blame others for their failings.

First comes the task of using these chances to your best advantage. The next step is timing, as you move forward from there. Without correct timing, even the most carefully planned projects—which may cost enormous amounts of money, energy and resources—come to naught.

It must be mentioned here that there are three stages in the completion process of any project. They are:

- The laying of the foundation plus the accumulation of all needed ingredients—resources, manpower and money
- The execution and careful development of the project
- The successful completion and enjoyment of rewards

Since the three stages are essential, at least the first item must be accomplished during the cycle of your favorable time. The meaningful commencement of a project, within the positive cycle, sets off a harmonious cycle for its growth that will continue even though the lucky time ceases.

If you carefully and methodically use this technique, achieving success becomes more a matter of technique rather than a stroke of luck, and you become in a small way the creator of your personal destiny.

Nature of Opportunities

Opportunity and *timing* play a key role in the process of creating success through personal efforts. Because we live on physical, mental and spiritual levels, life presents us with opportunities for the development of each. What we are saying is that material prosperity cannot be achieved within a spiritual cycle, which happens to be in a higher dimension. Needless to say, we must not mistake the material cycle for the spiritual.

Opportunity is not universal, even during our lucky streak. That is, a specific, given opportunity may be conducive to achieving a certain goal, but not conducive to achieving all goals. For instance, an aspiring actor may be offered a desirable lead role in a major movie, but this does not necessarily mean that this will improve his family life, love life, his social image or his health.

From the above example, it is quite clear that we need opportunities of various kinds. The next point is timing, without which the execution of a project, within the life of the greatest opportunity, may remain just a wish.

An opportunity may occur in a business, social, political, global, personal, or religious environment. A clash of opportunities may occur because of some contradiction in their nature. For instance, candidacy for a position in a political party may require sacrificing some family commitments of great importance. This would mean that the candidate has to make certain choices and compromises, because his or her political progress would amount to ignoring the family interests to a certain degree. "Clashing opportunities" often appear at the most strategic phases of human life. And, however you choose, the choice of one or the other may, one day, seem to have been a mistake.

Mind you, during the span of a good or positive cycle, anything attempted is likely to succeed, whatever the person's level of intelligence and application. This can give one a false sense of superiority if it continues over some time, for, as soon as the positive cycle comes to an end, the same person will not do so well, even in the same project.

Positive vibrational impact of planets increases the perceptive quality plus the reflex-action timing of a person, and these contribute largely to success. For example, if the person is, by nature, no good at real estate, but enters a positive cycle temporarily and goes into real estate, then by force of the cycle, he will tend to make money. This might make him think, wrongly, that he is an expert in real estate.

Such positive cycles influence all people at times, and could give one a very false sense of skill that could lead to ultimate disaster. As soon as the positive cycle ceases, this hapless person will start to make tactical mistakes because he does not have the basic knowledge. This happens many times in the case of stock market gurus, who make headlines for a little while. I have encountered these pundits, who did not have a thorough understanding and grasp of the basic astrological rules with which to give reliable and dependable advice on the stock market. Excellence is very rare.

You must take the plunge and do the work in order to find the pearls of wisdom.

Questions and Answers

Q: *When you say "a good cycle" or "a bad cycle," what do you mean? Do you mean that during a good cycle, I can get good results in a project no matter what I do?*

A: Suppose your project was started at a point A in your high energy period, but because of the length of the project, you have now entered a lower energy phase. What can you do to make sure that the project shall not fail for lack of the energy needed to reach a successful completion? There are a few things that can be done to replace your energy as it wanes when you yourself move into a lower-energy phase.

   • You could hire talented, younger people for your staff, who have the necessary energy and enthusiasm. Remember, your greatest asset at this stage is your life's experiences.

   • You could speed up the process of completion so that you don't enter the lowest energy phase when your senses will start to fail.

- You could set a mental target date, so that you can enjoy the success and thrill of the completed project ahead of time, and draw energy from that. Remember, however, that you must not be forced to compromise your values, and that the standard of your project's performance should not fall. Making sure in which energy phase you are, and will be in, is one of the most vital and necessary factors in determining whether or not you will succeed in a project.

These points are of prime importance when dealing with a financial venture. The future of your family will be tied into your own. And you would not like their hopes dashed because of your miscalculations or stupidity or carelessness. You would not like to disappoint them, would you?

Q: Do you have a solid basis for what you say, or are your utterances merely hypothetical? Have you had a chance to put to the test what you are preaching in this book?

A: Yes, I have made sure, by verifying my theories, that they do work. They are not just ideas; they are based on a firm footing. My many clients bear witness to the accuracy of my predictions for more than twenty years.

Anyone who takes the trouble to check the formulas contained in this book, by putting them to a test, will be rewarded with success after a reasonable amount of time and effort, depending upon the nature of the project and its complexity. This book is written for the doers who have the guts and the courage to take chances in life by trying out new ideas. I have outlined some techniques of success in this work that were used by some of the greatest occultists of the nineteenth and twentieth centuries, who were advisers to kings. And, remember that, in those days, the penalty for a wrong prognostication of the king's future was death!

Q: Can we create or attract our own opportunities or are they all a matter of luck? Do you simply have to be at the right place at the right time?

A: Some of us do create our own opportunities, especially those who have learned the art. If I went for an interview for a secretarial position but mentioned to the interviewer that I like to take responsibilities and can be relied upon and he is looking for a manager, he might say, "I like your personality and your attitude. I am going to give you a chance as a management trainee." In this instance I succeeded in creating an opportunity. But in most cases we attract our opportunities as a result of what we have done in the past, or what we can show others that we can do.

My definition of good luck is: A state of circumstances in which a person is in harmony with the electromagnetic forces or charges in his or her own orbit. Since most actions are preceded by thoughts (conscious or unconscious), very little happens as a matter of chance. It is very rare that an angel from heaven will guide me to a hidden treasure. Well-directed thoughts are often the hidden preamble to a happy episode and good luck.

Q: All life seems to move in cycles. Do good and bad cycles always alternate? How can we prepare for the bad ones well in advance?

A: Life does move in cycles, but good and bad cycles may or may not alternate. Before we can answer all these questions we have to understand what we are trying to find out. To the best of my knowledge, there is no one cycle that is good for all departments of life. During a good cycle a person may find love but his health may not necessarily improve. At times we are under the influence of more than one cycle (one good, one bad). The result will be dependent upon which one is the stronger of the two.

The duration of certain cycles is longer than others. This means that within the life of a major cycle we may have a minor cycle in operation, one contradicting the other. Very marked results may be expected when both the cycles are positive or vice versa.

Sometimes cycles alternate. Astrologically speaking, most of the major cycles can be calculated well in advance and we can thus be prepared in advance to deal with them. This is the wisest course to take. Calculating the timing of the bad or negative cycles gives us an opportunity to prepare for them long beforehand, especially if they tend to affect major areas of our life: health, profession or our love life. Since it takes time and effort to rearrange our financial and social circumstances, we must have enough time at hand to fully benefit from the warning. Sometimes even a minor cycle can wipe out most of the clout of a person in a short span of time and the negative results can be incalculable.

We hardly realize the value of such a warning, since it might save the entire future of all persons connected with the individual. Consciousness is a very valuable thing, whether we realize it or not. It is highly recommended to have most of the cycles in our lives calculated for all people in our family by a competent astrologer and to pay careful heed to the advice given. This can save you many disappointments, and even save what you deem most dear in your life.

The two faces of fate

In a positive cycle, unforeseen opportunities of two types will appear in the most mysterious manner. Some are predictable, while others are most unpredictable, arising under very strange circumstances. In a negative cycle this process will be reversed: Difficulties will present themselves at some expected times, while others will creep up when you least expect them, in a most unpredictable manner. Like a fire, explosion, outbreak of war, or an accident. Your property might suddenly need repairs. Other people's karma or cycle may be responsible, at certain times, for a positive or a negative event.

It is very hard to trace the cause of a positive or negative event— it can be a direct result of your personal efforts or someone else's karmic cycle. A gift may fall in your lap in the shape of money without your having done anything to deserve it, on a conscious level. Those of us who dream about a friend's or lover's success, are actually aiding him or her in materializing it. Not all laurels or crosses we bear are the direct result of our own efforts, but we choose to make ourselves responsible for them. There are forces in the unseen responsible for at least some of our successes and failures.

Q: Why are people more inclined to be helpful when we have a good cycle?
A: A good or a positive cycle brings about physiological changes, improving the magnetic faculty of the person, that make him or her more attractive to the outward stimuli, so that other people are drawn to him or her, and are more ready and willing to cooperate to help realize their dreams.

Conversely, while a person is in a negative cycle, other people are repulsed, and those who do remain in the orbit of the person concerned often end up hurting the person in a practical way by giving bad advice or suggestions.

Success in life depends largely upon our judgment of people and situations. Positive cycles improve our reflexes and the judgment faculty of the brain, thereby making us more receptive and conscious of opportunities which people do not normally notice or act upon. Even the most popular people, during the lifetime of a negative cycle, become unpopular and even their best friends may turn into enemies by vibrational impact. Then they fail to understand why the world has so turned against them, but it is only a matter of vibrational impact created by the influence of the negative cycle and nothing else.

Q: *How does timing influence the outcome of a project?*

A: This question may sound very simple on the surface but it is one of the key factors in determining the successful outcome of a project. When we launch an important project and ignore its correct timing, the chances of success are reduced considerably. A movie costing a few million dollars, with a great cast, camera man and director all doing their best work, if released at the wrong time, may not be a commercial success. Sometimes, a re-release, years later, brings success denied to the first showing.

A wrong time may be defined as a set of such circumstances as are not conducive to success in that particular project, and moving ahead in a wrong time will, almost always, produce poor results. It will certainly produce results less satisfactory than the same move made at a good time.

Figure 7 will be of great assistance to you in determining the state of health, mental condition and other factors which are the result of where you are in your development and which will let you see how all that affects your possible choices. It also makes clear that the assets and abilities upon which you chiefly rely may, and often do, change as you move on in years. This is often overlooked in less-well-laid plans for our old age, by people who wrongly, assume that certain skills and abilities are theirs for a whole lifetime.

Time and tide wait for no man.

—ENGLISH PROVERB

 # Karma Yoga— Yoga of Action

Avoid what is evil; do what is good; purify the mind;
this is the teaching of the Awakened One (Buddha).
—PALI CANON *SUTTAPITAKA DHAMMAPADA, CHAPTER 1, VERSE 14:183*

Our civilization provides so many conveniences that we have almost become slaves to them. We seem to expect someone else to take care of all our problems on the material and spiritual planes. We enjoy television, washing machines, radios, calculators, computers, cars, hot and cold running water, telephones, and lately, cell phones, electricity, gas, refuse collection and welfare programs; these are just a few of the things we like in our lives. We hardly realize how many things are done for us, and we have become so used to being served by someone else that we rarely notice when it is done.

Only if the service is interrupted, do we notice. We enjoy all this, but it has a negative aspect. These modern conveniences have softened us, made us too lazy to think and act for ourselves. They have stilled our reflexes because we use those less and less. And our affluent society has given rise to psychological pressures of various kinds that cause psychic complications, and only the very healthy people can survive.

Even though our material needs are fulfilled, what about our goals on the spiritual plane and our karmic debt?

Before we discuss that, I must state that I believe in reincarnation. In our present incarnation we bring with us our accumulated actions of the past incarnations and inherit certain faculties from our parents, but we always possess a free will. This is of paramount importance, because without a free will, evolution of the soul would be impossible to attain. All this means a lot of work needs to be done in this life. Only our positive actions can help us work out our previous karma.

An Indifferent Attitude to the Future

Whether God exists or not is debatable, say some people. In some nations, there are people who do not pay much attention to prayers, although they are considered prosperous in every way. People in these nations may be materially well-off, but what about their intellectual and spiritual growth?

When we become indifferent to an existing problem, we may repress conscious thoughts about it, yet it continues to bother us and manifests as frustration, an irritable attitude, or ultimately, feelings that our intellectual and spiritual needs are unfulfilled, which we still sense, even if only unconsciously.

Let us examine how a success-oriented person thinks and the way a failure-oriented person does. See figure 9, Positives and Negatives.

There is a lot of misunderstanding about the Hindi word *karma*, meaning our accumulated deeds in this and former lives and their effect on our future lives. Because we have a free will, we can change our way of thinking and thus alter our karma. By changing our thinking from negative to positive, our actions will also change for the better. Thus, we conclude that thinking is destiny. Millions of people all over the world have thought that. Since we are all free, we must each take the initiative and perform right actions. No one else can do this for us—not a spouse, not a lover, not a priest, not even God.

Some people do not have the courage to fight the existing circumstances; as a result, they continue to suffer. In such cases prayer truly helps. I have noticed that most people who are in a rut often lack the courage to risk change, or they do not trust themselves sufficiently to take a chance and try to improve themselves and their lot. A poor self-image, mental and physical lethargy and a pessimistic outlook are generally the underlying causes that have made a person fatalistic or defeatist.

Figure 9
Positives and Negatives

Success-oriented person	Failure-oriented person
• Seeks adventure	• Has anxiety
• Has ambition	• Finds arguments for failure
• Anticipates good things	• Expects bad things to happen
• Argues against failure	• Feels depressed
• Thrives on business	• Faces obstacles in business
• Has cheerfulness leading to good health	• Has pessimism leading to disease
• Comforts of living well (thinks of)	• Is resigned to being poor
• Has self-confidence	• Lacks self-confidence
• Concentrates on projects at hand	• Procrastinates
• Has consciousness	• Is absent-minded
• Displays courage	• Is afraid
• Criticizes in a positive way	• Finds fault with everything
• Has determination	• Is undecided
• Pays heed to personal development	• Ignores personal weaknesses and limitations
• Uses discrimination for efficiency and success	• Is indiscriminate while looking for reasons to fail
• Is enterprising	• Lacks enterprise
• Has full faith in future and self	• Has a lack of faith in self and others
• Has right success-producing habits	• Has wrong habits that produce failure
• Is happy at most times	• Is mostly unhappy and miserable
• Likes most things	• Hates most things
• Is helpful to others	• Is indifferent to the needs of others
• Is usually honest	• Is mostly dishonest
• Is idealistic	• Lacks ideals
• Has idols and role models	• Has no idols, does not learn by example
• Is intelligent and introspective	• Lacks intelligence and introspection
• Thinks of riches and prosperity	• Thinks of poverty and privation
• Is confident of success	• Engages in self-pity
• Visualizes success	• Is confident of failure
• Is masterful	• Is slavish
• Is active	• Is sluggish
• Has initiative	• Always waits for orders; no initiative
• Has dynamic thoughts	• Has static thoughts
• Has strong self-esteem	• Has self-distrust
• Is assertive	• Retreats—doesn't advance
• Has continuity of purpose	• Is fickle

There is no easy solution to resolving a negative past karma, but a carefully planned step-by-step course of action does indeed help a great deal. Mind you, simply having problems does not necessarily make you a past-life sinner. We face problems because of others' folly, through mistakes of our own, or because of the lessons we must learn. It may sound strange, but it is true.

Many people think that the guru (a spiritual teacher) should help them work out their karma. Certain yogis do take on the karma of their disciples, but this is not generally done. Nor, if done, does it always help the student. Imagine a doting mother who falls down, so that her child, in the process of learning to walk, won't hurt himself. What would that child ever learn?

Can any karmic debts be written off?

As I understand the natural laws, we must each repay our karmic debts. But God is the final judge. He has a reputation for being merciful and kind to those who repent. The God-realized gurus (like very seasoned attorneys) are familiar with natural laws and can teach one how to avoid paying the debt in full. In certain cases they help the disciple work out his or her past karma so that future development can move ahead, unobstructed.

Remember, a totally bankrupt man gets no credit. If our past accounts are not settled, we cannot expect to make much progress. And one's past karma keeps on compounding, just as interest fees weigh down the debtor's ability to repay.

Why wait? Make things happen

Let us examine why things happen the way they do in life and what we should do to carve out a new and better future. There are certain basics we must understand before we can make things happen according to our own wish. The knowledge of certain natural laws and their application are the prerequisites. They are our awareness that even in the periods of greatest stress the law of karma (of action and reaction) does operate with great precision. It means that if John and Gordon both have an unlucky spell, they will not suffer equally. Why? Simply because John may work harder than Gordon against all odds and overcome the negative influences by his personal concerted efforts, thus nullifying to a large extent the negative vibrations. It must also be remembered that our physical, mental and spiritual makeup greatly decide the extent to which we must suffer as a result of unfavorable conditions. For instance, persons born with their Sun in the earth signs, in Taurus (April 21 to May 21) or Virgo (August 24 to September 23) or Capricorn (December 23 to January 20) tend to suffer, physically, more than say, a person born in the air sign Libra (September 24 to October 23). This is because in a general way, the air signs have more willpower than the earth signs.

Persons who are mostly on the mental or spiritual plane, who are already "on the path," have the capability to work out their karma with much greater ease. A corollary to this is that the more materially advanced people are, generally, the less enlightened they are. That's why we have so few "chiefs" and so many "Indians." Those who are capable of being leaders are few. Natural-born followers are abundant.

To move ourselves forward, we should face all our problems boldly. This simply means that the will to win must not weaken, no matter how bad things look. When we persistently cling to a positive image, even when surrounded by negative influences for a long time, our subconscious mind brings into reality that positive image in spite of everything. That's why some great men find it hard to believe that they are defeated, even when they actually have lost the fight and why others, after a defeat, can make a comeback and achieve success again.

The next point is quite important, but before I go further, I must mention here, that when we are more persistent than the problem itself, we are victorious over it. Should we not defeat the problem, we will surely be defeated by it. Remember, most people don't use more than 10 percent of their brain cells. They fail to discover their full potential, and they settle for an ordinary life.

Whose fault is that? If we don't move a muscle, we can't blame fate, God, society, the government, the capitalists, the politicians, our parents or our siblings for our poor results. Many people have the wrong-headed notion that the world owes them a living. This is not so.

There are two ways of leading a life: One is to accept the crumbs given by fate without complaint. The second is to make an effort, or lots of efforts—whatever it takes—to earn the right to possess the good things of life. Most people can do much better than they do, but they don't really try, because they accept a poor self-image implanted by society, circumstances or parents, and they believe a mediocre life is their only possible destiny. Thus, they are miserable, unhappy and unsuccessful by choice (conscious or unconscious), not by Godly design.

Nature is neutral and impartial. It punishes no one. But we punish ourselves, frequently. A non-observance of natural laws leads to wrong actions which in turn leads to failure; that's when the strong person starts over, or tries his attack at a different angle. He doesn't quit, is the point.

We should make our best efforts to change our fate (the sum total of all our actions past and present) by taking positive and constructive steps. It is vital to do the best we can, no matter how small the job might be. Trifles make perfection, and perfection is no trifle. We can learn a great deal from nature. For instance, look at a flower. Each and every petal is uniquely and perfectly formed. We can align ourselves with nature by making our actions positive and constructive. In the mind of God, all creation is one.

Our plans must include the welfare of others in a constructive way. Selfless action is considered to be the best because selfishness always leads to errors of judgment. It is not without reason that God-realized gurus are selfless and unmoved by what happens to the world. They are not indifferent (indifference is the greatest sin), but knowing better, they are reluctant to interfere with the functions of creation. "Conquer your problems with the power within you" and "continue always to look ahead." These old maxims spell out how you can make all your plans successful.

Why wait? Make things happen. The time is NOW. The one who waits for things to happen never gets anywhere. Inaction is very damaging—physically, mentally and spiritually. Care must be taken to channel your energies in positive and constructive ways. And care must be taken to formulate our plans in accordance with the laws of nature. All nature moves forward. Those who are too selfish to care about others' interests are in error. It is more blessed to give than to receive. For instance, enlightened souls such as gurus do not accept any gifts. Why? For the simple reason that all things we attain have their karma attached to them. And a guru doesn't want your bad karma messing up his.

If I unethically extracted a hundred dollars from a person, that money would carry an evil karma with it, and anyone who receives that money will not be able to enjoy it. Even if I were to give that money to charity, the receiving party will not be able to make much use of it because the bad karma is still with it.

Why? Because those hundred dollars would shrink to minimum effectiveness. Are you aware that hard-earned money stretches? Think about it. Money made by unethical means carries a very bad karma. That is why robbers, thieves and extortionists are always poor in the long run.

Make things happen—starting today—by doing positive things and aligning yourself with the forces of good. Be active mentally, physically and spiritually. Keep the forces of nature on your side.

What do you want to be? Most people wrongly believe that higher goals are hard to achieve. But this is not exactly true. By "higher goals" we may not necessarily mean greater material wealth. Attaining intellectual wealth requires a different type of effort.

Whatever you are, at whatever age, you are in one stage of life, and you can create desired changes by following a certain procedure. Nature itself is impartial to the cycles and patterns that move within it. By decreasing our emphasis on materialistic things to emphasize a more spiritualistic way of thinking, and by setting different (better) priorities, we change our lives, and can achieve more contentment and lasting happiness. And it is never too late. When a king gives away all his wealth to the poor and seeks the wisdom of the sages, he is, in fact, moving himself to a higher state of development.

Most of us are so materially content or indifferent to our present circumstances, that the thought of moving to a higher, more spiritual realm never appears in our minds. But, if we wish to make progress, we must have a thorough knowledge of where we exactly stand— what are our achievements on material, intellectual and spiritual levels in the past, what are our limitations, and expectations, and just which goals we must set for the future.

Inactivity and Fate

To be a fatalist does not mean you can leave everything to an external agency, or that you can avoid putting personal effort into fighting life's problems. Inaction in every shape and form constitutes laziness, and is highly injurious to one's life prospects. If my house were on fire and, instead of trying to put it out, I merely looked on and cursed fate for punishing me, my wrong-headed indifference would show my reluctance to face and defeat adversity. Indifference here could more properly be called "sloth."

When Smith's family had nothing to eat, he did not try to earn bread to feed the family, and he did not curtail his regular whisky consumption. Instead, he had two whiskies, so he could forget his problems. Yet, he expected the tide would turn in his favor "someday".

Fate favors the ones who try hard, who get up and "go do," who are quite willing to earn their good fortune, not accept it as alms. Benjamin Franklin was the fifteenth of seventeen children of a poor candlemaker. He had only one year of schooling. He taught himself philosophy, four languages, the classics, finance and politics. He became one of the best educated and greatest Americans.

Are some people actually lazy? Perhaps fatalists are, to a degree, and become more so by virtue of their wrong mental attitudes and circumstances. But every man is quite free to alter his circumstances; he does not have to put up with apparent lethargy and inertia. Deep down in each of us is a natural urge to rise and perfect oneself.

It improves nothing to blame our parents or society, or even our luck when, by conscious or unconscious indifference we miss out on rare opportunities or misuse them. We cannot blame others for all the twists and turns of our fate. People who think the world owes them a living are in a fool's paradise. This earth is not an hotel—it is a battlefield. You get out of life what you put into it. And we all must work for what we want. There is no such thing as "What will be, will be." Not without effort.

Yes, what will be *will* be—if people carry on without growing up, and without accepting responsibility for what happens to them. If they do not change their ways before it is too late, you can see such people as they come to the end of life, doubting every truth they come across, suspecting all sincere persons they meet, rejecting and discouraging those who may still have some loyalty or wish to help them. It must be mentioned here that it is desire that binds a soul to the earth. We have many incarnations in order to undo any wrongs we may have done while on earth, and settle all accounts with those we meet.

Intellectual Facets of Desire and Rebirth

By doing things ourselves we find answers to some of life's intricate problems. Actions can be performed on a physical, mental or spiritual plane. It is true that "they also serve who only stand and wait," as Milton said. The results of any deed can be realized, usually on the plane upon which the action was performed. In the case of visualization (action on the mental plane) the desire may be realized on the physical plane, depending upon what is visualized, and how effective one is at putting one's true emotion into the visualizing process.

Because most people choose to perform only the physical actions, while totally ignoring their mental or spiritual potential, their latent mental and spiritual faculties never get a chance to develop and be put to good use for the betterment of the individual or of the world. Trying to attain direct results quickly, these people forget that the physical plane is much inferior to the mental or spiritual. Strange as it may seem, more than 75 percent of the time most of us are trying to please our fickle senses.

If the satisfaction of a desire on the physical plane were to give rise to, say, two new desires, at the rate of one thousand desires per year, we would have some twenty thousand desires to be satisfied in a span of just twenty years. Those, in turn, would give birth to forty thousand new desires.

What a mess we would create in a lifetime! Or during a few lifetimes (if we believe in reincarnation). And we have completely forgotten our desires on the mental and spiritual planes and how long it could take to realize those.

Suppose the total number of desires of a person is one hundred thousand in one life, and it takes one year to relinquish one desire completely. It would take one hundred thousand earthly years to get rid of all of them. And if we take fifty years as an average life span, that would mean two thousand lives a person will have to live, simply to satisfy all those physical-plane desires.

What do you spend time thinking about? Because mental action is of such a superior quality, saints and sages work out most of their own karma on the mental plane, ignoring the physical realm (Oh!

What a relief!) and thus not only outwit other mortals, but out-produce them as well.

How You Can Become Rich!

If you would like to be rich and successful, you have to be ambitious; you have to have a dream. Mr. N.M., the millionaire president of a famous baseball team, is of the opinion that you have to have the desire to be the greatest artist there ever was, the top industrialist or the best civic leader. He's right in at least one respect: You are very unlikely to become rich by accident.

You must aim very high. Mediocre wishes don't pay off. If you aim at the presidency of the United States, you might end up becoming a senator or state governor. But dreams are not enough, dreams only come true through hard work. There is one universal trait all successful people have: They were not afraid of hard work and putting in long hours.

Intelligence and imagination are both very important to help you come up with the right ideas for yourself and to work out a plan of action, but even the greatest ideas are no good in a vacuum. They must be put to practical use. To build up a thriving business takes a great deal of dedication, but if you think you have the capacity and are ready to invest your time, money and energy in your project, without in the beginning worrying about the results, you certainly are on the right track.

Questions and Answers

Q: *If a person does not believe in reincarnation and past karma, how do you explain why some are born wealthy and others, poor?*

A: Your question is based on the assumption that there is no reincarnation. In this particular context, poverty and wealth will take on different coloring. Even if we deny the concept of re-incarnation, life would be, as we know it, impossible without any distant or recent past. I explain: The duration of the split second of the eternal "now" in which we are able to do anything is not that long, comparatively speaking. We can only do something in the present. And any accumulation of all our actions of this present will become our fate.

It is correct to say that people are born into a poor or wealthy family. It will be appropriate to say that no one is born utterly poor because all possess the potential to create wealth at will, with personal effort, and materialize it on a physical plane.

Let me clarify a very vital and key point here. The Western civilization is extroverted while the Eastern is introverted. In the West, people believe only in what they can see on the physical plane. When we look at a building, we don't notice the foundation on which it stands, but that foundation must exist in order that the building may stand.

We have become oblivious of the fact that a human being is not only the physical body with a very coarse vibration (a lower frequency rate) but is also endowed with a mind and a soul. The manifest form of God was brought about by the concentration of God's thought held there by His infinite will. But there are other worlds more wonderful and greater in size than our small world.

Back to our subject. As long as a person has an intellect (and everyone has), physical prowess and a soul, he is not truly poor. Poverty and wealth are two concepts assumed by the Western civilization long ago. We tend to measure wealth by the amount of money in the bank. We are not aware that money does not exist by itself, but is merely a means of exchange. The barter system was in operation long before we started to mint coins. We have to re-learn our definitions if we want to change our present concept of poverty or wealth. If one person makes $10,000 a year and another makes $100,000, is the first one poor? These things are relative.

It is a grave mistake to judge the whole person only by the money he currently has. We should instead study the picture in its entirety. Measure the intellectual, spiritual and material achievements of a person before labeling him or her "poor" or "wealthy." The one who possesses higher faculties on the mental and spiritual planes has graduated to a much higher dimension and craves success on those planes rather than hankering after physical plane perishables, which have no ultimate reality. Life is matter of consciousness and realization. A saint, having understood the constitution of the universe, grieves no more to the changing scenes of pleasure and pain that he notices everyday.

A person being made in the image of the almighty God is not born poor. It is our wrong beliefs that are responsible for wrong opinions. If you think you are poor, it means you believe yourself to be poor. How can that be? It violates all the laws of abundance that flows eternally from God. We are all children of God, and hence entitled to all good things like happiness and prosperity—but we must each make our claim by making an effort. Even God has to make efforts, so why not you or me?

Q: To what extent are major events in life predestined?
A: Your question implies that you believe in destiny. The seeds of whatever circumstances and conditions we face today were sown by us through our actions in the immediate or distant past. If we sow carrots, we get carrots. I believe that cycles, both short and long, positive and negative, have a great bearing upon our lifestyles, and our happiness or sorrow.

What is a major event? It will have a different meaning to different people, and each meaning will depend upon our set of values. Loss or gain of a material object is one definition, loss or gain of honor is another, loss of a loved one, another. Major events, of necessity, must fall in a strong cycle (when forces are at their maximum) so they can have full effect.
Sometimes a cycle with a short span may produce the most important results for better or worse. I have noticed that a major (long) cycle may sometimes pass without any important event taking place. It is the strength of a cycle and a concurrence of circumstances that crystallize out into particular events. They are only pre-destined in the sense that an event will come or not, according to our actions of the past, and any seeds sown must sprout at the right time. This is in keeping with the law.

Q: Some people never seem to get a break in life no matter how hard they try. Is this related to destiny?
A: There could be two possibilities here: either the person in some

distant past has continuously violated most of the natural laws or totally ignored or not availed himself or herself of all the opportunities that came along. Destiny is nothing but an accumulation of the results of all our actions good or bad. It is not correct to say that some people never get a break. According to the law of action and reaction, destiny can be created through action, and an accumulation of positive actions must bring good results one day, just as we have to pay for our wrong actions by suffering. I have noticed in some cases that a person has had a run of negative cycles for five or ten years, but in a span of human life, say of seventy years, a ten-year bad cycle still only means one-seventh.

Our mental and physiological makeup greatly determines our reaction to all the breaks we get, but should there be certain blocks in the mental make-up of a person, then they will let the opportunities pass by without even being recognized, and that person will never take advantage of the opportunities that were in fact there, because the person concerned never "saw" them. It is a matter of being conscious of the opportunity and then reacting to it appropriately. When the opportunity is of a short duration, the person must react to it very quickly to make the most of it, especially in those cases where the number of opportunities for personal advancement happen to be very few in the entire life.

Q: There are many great people like Helen Keller or Abraham Lincoln, who battled against unfavorable circumstances. How were they able to overcome such adverse conditions?

A: These people were of a very high caliber, and were born with a tremendous degree of willpower to overcome any obstacles or unfavorable circumstances they had to face. Great people of the earth never view difficulties as such, but consider them as challenges to their will, to be faced boldly with persistence and determination. Needless to say, their will is an iron will and can easily surmount whatever hindrances may lie in their paths. All such people have a mission to fulfill and it is that sense of mission that acts as a driving force, that inspires them and impels them to perform great deeds to help humanity and to alleviate its suffering. Adversities only appear to be negative on a physical plane, but the flip side is, they are the best soul cleansers. Looking at these two people from what we have just said, these two great personages set a good example for the rest of humanity to follow and that is: never give up in the face of difficulties.

Fix your mind on Me, be devoted to Me, worship Me and bow to Me; so shall you without doubt reach Me. This I truly promise you; for you are dear to Me.
    —Lord Krishna, *Bhagavad Gita*, Ch. XVIII, 65

We can do anything we want to do if we stick to it long enough.
    —Helen Adams Keller

How People Who Surround You Can Make or Break You

6

Fate chooses our relatives, we choose our friends.
—JACQUES DE LILLE, *MALHEUR ET PITIÉ*, CANTO I

There are two types of people in our lives: right people and wrong people. No one is right for all time and for every project or relationship. A person will enter your orbit, play his or her role, good or bad, then soon disappear from the scene. Flux is the nature of creation. We must accept changes in our lives or perish. From the time we are born, we are surrounded by people, yet very few remain with us for a major part of our lives. This is a very deep topic involving karmic relationships.

Some people are attracted to us, and others are repelled. Some help us, while others hinder. Some stay in our orbit for five years, others for ten years, and some few play a key role throughout the entire span of our lives. Those who harmonize on the material plane help us materialize our dreams, while others stimulate us mentally or spiritually. People with a set of moral values contradictory to ours will disturb our psychic balance by vibrational conflict. See figure 10, Man and his orbit.

The total amount of success in our lives will largely depend upon the people who surround us. How do people influence us? We each have an energy field surrounding our body. When we come within the limits of the other person's energy field (the person's aura), a vibrational exchange takes place. When the energies exchanged are positive, they induce in both parties positive thoughts and impulses, which can prove most beneficial to both. When there is a clash of positive and negative energies, the results can be very harmful. If A is very positive, and B is negative, due to B's negative influence, A will begin to think negatively, thus temporarily impairing his judgment.

Figure 10
Man and His Orbit

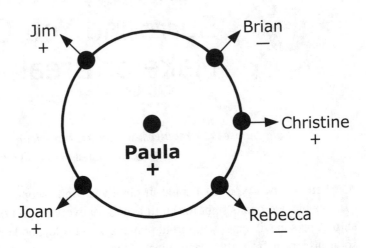

Figure 10: From our very childhood, we are surrounded by people. Some are attracted to us while others are repulsed. Positive persons prove very productive and help us realize our aims but negative people become a hindrance and impede our progress. The more people we have who are positive, the better it is for us. A positive vibrational exchange creates harmony between people involved. This creates attraction as a result of happiness. Yes, happiness attracts and misery repels.

We can change our orbit of people surrounding us by analysis and replacing each negative person by a positive one, thereby increasing our chances of success and prosperity manifold.

Everything in life moves in cycles, but we also have to contend with conditions created by the people or animals in our individual or several orbits. Generally speaking it is pretty difficult to remove a person from a particular orbit. Just as the removal of one molecule from the structure will totally change the composition of a substance, in the same manner, removal of negative influences could make a person more successful materially and even bring about positive genetic changes.

The substitution process will involve replacing each negative person from our orbit by a positive person thereby changing the composition of the orbit that will trigger positive events in the future by vibrational impact. Negative people always trigger cataclysmic events in the lives of those surrounding them that may have an epicenter. Participants of an event are pulled by a magnetic force very hard to resist.

Depending on the type of influence, a person's vibrations can make us violent or romantic. When two people come into contact, a struggle takes place between the positive and negative forces. Initially the positive forces will resist the influence of the negative.

A strongly negative person is almost certain to take over the aura of a more positive person. Once the negative person has taken over the other person's aura completely, the resistance will cease, and the "victim" will become resigned, and start imitating the negative person's ways of thinking. This occurs in a very subtle fashion. We see examples of this happening in the animal kingdom, where lions hypnotize their prey, and the prey struggles no more. Snakes do it, too. Rabbits or deer that get caught in the headlights of an oncoming car are unable to move, as if hypnotized.

The Human Biomagnetic Energies:

Plants, animals, bacteria and man all have different bio-magnetic energies. Every living thing transmits from its body certain electromagnetic energies. These energies, also called magnetic fluids, have great impact on other human beings. World leaders who have very large biomagnetic fields, influence nations many miles away in a positive or negative way. The range of these energies can be almost unlimited.

Mankind is affected by incoming electromagnetic energies, such as those coming from outer space, the moon, the sun, and the other major planets.

The moon affects the rise and fall of the tides, as does the sun; and when the moon's and the sun's energies are combined, they act to exert their maximum pull on the earth, producing abnormally high tides.

Man, like all living biological systems, experiences changes in these pulls as strains and stresses that are a result of these bodies from outer space and their electromagnetic fields and gravitational forces. He is an electromagnetic animal and is subject to those forces that affect all forms of life existing on earth. Man's electromagnetic system is contained within his biophysical makeup and affects the total behavior of not only his body but also in many cases, causes changes in his mental activities and the electrical biochemical operation of his entire system.

Man is continually bombarded with visible and invisible electromagnetic energies that have direct bearing on life, mental attitudes, health and welfare.

The greatest effective generators of harmful, as well as useful and healthful energies are the rays of the sun. The sun's rays are electromagnetic in nature and effects.

Note: These energies must not be confused with the human aura. Zone of influence of the Aura is limited, but that of biomagnetism is relatively unlimited.

The human aura can be seen by clairvoyants. This subtle invisible emanation from the human body can be photographed with Kirlian photography, which clearly show the inner and outer auras. The colors vary according to the mental and physical states of the entire being.

People in our surroundings have a tremendous influence on our mental health and indirectly affect our physical and spiritual well-being. Or, if their influence be highly negative or evil, it may destroy us and our lives. Rasputin's evil influence upon the Czar of Russia and his daughter brought about the downfall of the Romanoff dynasty. Rasputin maneuvered the czar's thinking and manipulated him in ways that were totally detrimental and disastrous to the political and social interests of Russia.

After Rasputin came into the czar's life, the czar could no longer think independently for himself or his country. He was under a negative spell that did not allow him to think clearly. So the czar made many poor tactical decisions, which made his people turn against him. A secret society was even formed to remove the czar and rid the country of the evil Rasputin.

We are not all czars, but success largely depends upon our choice of right people and right geographical location. The greater the number of right people surrounding us, the greater will be our success and harmony. See figure 11, the success formula.

What Characterizes Right and Wrong People?

We recognize the right people through our first intuitive feelings about them. If our feelings about a person in the first meeting are negative, we should not ignore this. It is a very basic defense mechanism, one that can cost us heavily if we ignore it. Sometimes, because of practical reasons, some people, who do not harmonize with us, still will become our close acquaintances, sometimes even our friends, but eventually the outcome will not be happy. We are greatly influenced by objects and people in our environment.

Figure 11
Success Formula

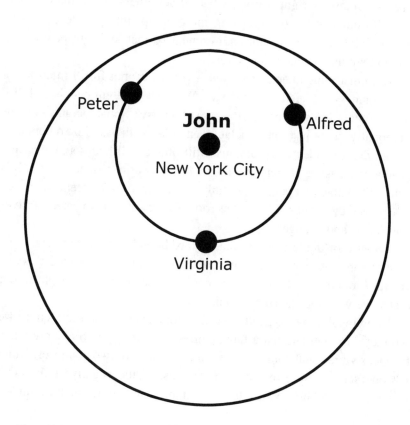

Figure 11: In the above figure, John has in his orbit Peter, Alfred and Virginia (each person here is in harmony with John individually, thereby creating the most conducive environment for success.) His location is New York City, assisted by the most propitious time attended by other success-producing elements (adequate amount of money, persistence, hard work and a positive mental attitude, etc.) then success is sure provided the venture has been carefully chosen.

And that, my friends, is the formula of success on a material plane.

The first step is to become conscious of the fact that we are affected by the vibrational impact of other people. The second would be to think what characterizes right people, what attracts them to us; then we can decide to concentrate on attracting more compatible people to us. We have to create a good mental environment so that the right people will wish to help us succeed in our aims.

You must remember that the same person cannot fulfill the roles of lover, business associate, and relative. We need different people to fulfill our different needs. This is the law of nature. Some people help us emotionally, some just make us laugh and play with us, while others help us with deep intellectual problems. Still others will help us evolve in a spiritual way, as we change and move through various stages of life. It is important to note that people naturally disappear from the scene once they have played their roles. This makes room for new people to enter our lives as we grow and change.

Because of the laws of karma, we are bound to meet both right and wrong people. As we grow in wisdom, we begin to understand this and will start looking for harmonious people. If we keep this thought in our minds, we will find the right people.

Knowing that we do need the right people, we should search until we find them. In international affairs, battles and even wars broke out when there was vibrational conflict between the leaders of two countries. Hitler was one such person, responsible for most of the negative things that transpired around him. World history is replete with other such examples.

How People Who Surround You, Can Make or Break You

From the time we are born, people surrounding us can truly make or break us. As infants we are totally dependent on our parents and, if we are unwelcome and unloved, we may be traumatized for life. Children who receive unconditional love and support from their parents have a much better chance to overcome the difficulties they face and to develop their full potential.

Once during one of my seminars on self-empowerment, I said to a lady sitting in the front row with a gentleman: "What would you do if I told you that this man is not good for you, vibrationally?"

"But Mr. Ostaro, I have nobody else," she retorted.

This is a typical example of how we compromise, and associate with wrong people as a matter of convenience, and sacrifice the rosy future that could be ours if only we would form new relationships with people who vibrate with us in a positive way. Mental laziness or lethargy can be very harmful, and a high price has to be paid. One may not achieve success in this lifetime; as a result of such poor choices, one may have to start again at the bottom of the ladder of development in a new life.

The most important thing is to find out who is right for us vibrationally and who is wrong. We should make it our business to analyze all people we associate with intimately, know which are good for us and which are not, and then systematically weed out the negative ones. It will be a painful process but it will give us wonderful and positive results in the future.

If you live in a family or in a country where social conditions are not congenial to you, move away from that society or country to a place where you have better chances of meeting, finding and enjoying the people who will support your views, aspirations and dreams.

I did just that. At a very early age I realized that my Indian family values, circumstances, traditions, and philosophy would never provide me full scope for my mental and spiritual development and help me in the evolution that was a part of my make-up. Impelled by all these thoughts, my rebellious spirit made a firm resolve to leave my homeland for good. I made a plan of action and nursed it with all the resources and forces at my command. I constantly pursued my aim, undeterred by all the evidence to the contrary, despite how many difficulties and rejections tried to dampen my resolve.

And one bright morning, I sailed from Bombay on a large, French ship, bound for Marseilles, France, without a friend and with very little money in my pocket and no knowledge of the French language. I did have an unflinching faith in God. Being anchored in God, every difficulty that I encountered was resolved as if by magic. Upon arriving in France I had to carve out a new life for myself.

I share part of my very private struggles so that you may be inspired by my story. Any man or woman can do what one man has done. So, my dear reader, learn from my example and never accept defeat in the battle of life.

Those people who have similar views, and who vibrate in harmony with you, will go out of their way to help you materialize your dreams, without worrying about how big the sacrifice is, or how much such a support would cost. Examples are plentiful: politicians (Republicans or Democrats, Whigs or Tories), and religious leaders (Catholics or Protestants), (Hindus or Muslims), (Jews or Gentiles), have invested time, effort and money to support their causes in history, and did not care what dreams the other factions had.

Great people change places and persons by intuition. You can do it by using analysis and thus become equally as successful. Don't compromise your personality or principles.

If you are not happy where you are, don't sit back nonchalantly: Do something about it. It is your life and future. If you want to go to heaven, it is you who must die and no one else.

But whether we receive full support and love from our parents does not entirely depend on their good will and material prosperity. Parents, although they profess to love all their children equally, tend to favor those with whom they are in vibrational harmony. Why does the naughty behavior of one child irritate us, while we tolerate the same behavior in another? A child who is in vibrational harmony with his father or mother will instinctively be more cooperative with that particular parent.

Even if you do not know much about astrology and the sign you were born under, you must have noticed that you feel more comfortable around people born in the same month or those born in a complementary sign. Popularly, we call it "being on the same wavelength." A person born in the sign of Aries (March 22 to April 20) will have certain characteristics, such as energy, courage and leadership qualities, which are complementary to someone born in the sign of Sagittarius (November 23 to December 22) or a person born in the royal sign of Leo (July 24 to August 23) who will be faithful, gracious and loyal. When we recognize traits in our children that are similar to our own, we will not only appreciate them if they be positive, but also condone them, if they be habits or weaknesses we can understand or relate to.

The Growing-up Orbit

If you grow up in a family where you have a conflict or poor vibration with both parents, you will rebel against the entire family, and all of your faculties and forces will operate to negate their ideas and opinions, even if this is self-destructive. A force applied to an aim in the reverse order, neutralizes its creativity and starts a negative cycle, producing failure-causing vibrations. You will do everything in the opposite way, against what such parents tell you to do, as a reaction to their imposition of their views and ways of doing things. This can result in a chain reaction leading to eventual disaster, for the person concerned, and much suffering.

If a child has a vibrational conflict with only one parent, then the harm (mental and physical) to the child could be somewhat lessened. It all depends upon the type of parents a child has. If the conflicting parent is stronger (vibrationally) than the parent who harmonizes with the child, the former will stamp the child's personality more than the latter. In this case, the good is neutralized by the negative. Since we consider our parents as role models, their personalities affect our mental make-up substantially. For example, if we are constantly told "where there is muck, there is money," we will start to consider money as a dirty thing.

An Aries father (born in April) is likely to conflict with his Libra (born in October) daughter and induce in her (by vibrational impact) contradictory qualities, like using force to get things done and having a pioneering spirit, as opposed to enjoying the peace and harmony which the Libra daughter is endowed with natively. The Libra daughter will react by becoming too overbearing and dictatorial, in order to survive a non-congenial vibrational imposition.

The Enigma of Vibrational Harmony

When two people are in harmony (in a positive way) it brings out the best in terms of thinking processes, including the discriminative faculty. When we harmonize with a person then we like that person because that person makes us happy. Happiness attracts and misery repels. That is why comedians are so popular. Liking creates attraction. We please those we like and do things for them even at the cost of great sacrifices and material expense. Harmony on a mental plane is stronger than on a physical plane. That's why millions had to go to the gallows in history; they were condemned due to mental inharmony with their kings. Physical harmony is temporary while mental is long-lasting.

A vibrational clash interferes with the judgment-making process of a person and makes the person do the wrong thing, despite his or her best intentions. Having good intentions and being able to put them into practice are two different things. Why do we make such mistakes? It is because all matter obeys the law of vibration. And we are nothing but matter. A vibrational conflict between two people will force them to make errors of judgement and that must reflect itself in wrong actions.

If you went to a surgeon for an operation and your vibrations were in conflict with him or her, he or she might make an incision at the wrong spot and may take out the wrong organ from your body. Can you imagine what you would be risking at wrong hands? I have purposely used "wrong" more than once for emphasis.

Mind you, a conflict of moral values is a lot more disastrous than simple physical vibrational differences. World history bears a witness to this fact. How many people have perished in conflicts between Catholics and Protestants, Jews and Gentiles, and other people of different religious beliefs and moral values? The enmity between Hindus and Muslims is a known fact and thousands have died from this conflict over the years. In the political arena, the harm done to people is usually on a national level and the consequences are on an international scale. The Communist leaders of the Soviet Union poured millions into India to convert the Indian populace to Communism, but it was of no avail since the Indian beliefs are rooted in religion. The repercussions of a political exercise of this nature have global consequences. What happens to one nation affects the rest of the world. Communist propaganda aimed at and force-fed to the world population in just this one century, has cost the world community many billions of dollars and impoverished many nations. As a result the cost of it has brought about the eventual break-up of the Soviet Union, since the colonies could not be fed with such a corrupt system, where every person in power had to be bribed in order for the people below to get the bare necessities of life.

A difference of opinion is a very fine thing if it does not impose restrictions on the freedom of thoughts and actions of others. The imposition of an opinion on a person or a people creates struggle and turmoil in the minds of those people whose different ideas we try to suppress. We have to learn to live with an opposing view, and keep both in balance. The red corpuscles are as essential as the white ones in the same body, and must co-exist. Duality is the nature of creation.

To get back to parenting: whenever the parents happen to be spiritual, their outlook on life will not hurt the evolution of the soul of the child as much as totally materialistic parents might. We do things for people we like.

Our family environment when we are growing up fixes our beliefs in people and things. If we experience hardship, cruelty, privation, restrictions and denial in the family as children, we can become bitter, angry and frustrated adults.

Child or adult, the choice of our close friends is very crucial because we share our very personal and private thoughts and beliefs with them, and their attitudes and opinions reinforce or conflict with ours.

Just as harmonious friends help us become good, helpful, sincere and loving, inharmonious friends induce in us negative traits (that may not be a part of our nature) like hatred, selfishness, meanness and indifference to suffering.

We should carefully choose people who surround us so that the total outcome of our lives is positive and we leave this earth a slightly better place than what we found it to be at birth.

Sometimes we say to ourselves: why do I feel this? Why am I reacting towards this person in such an unfriendly manner? The answer is that our whole being reacts extremely to any situation which is directly opposed to our own "atmosphere" (the sum total of all the three bodies: physical, ideational and astral). Here, opposition to the alien "other" is necessary. Whenever a person tries to impose (by vibrations) something upon another person of a totally different constitution, the result will be a very strong resistance or non-acceptance of the vibrations of the person who is trying to impose his or her personality.

A hostile or a turbulent home atmosphere is not healthy and does not help a child achieve proper growth and develop the various faculties of his or her mind. A negative atmosphere at home can turn a mentally healthy and well adjusted child into an outlaw or a social criminal. If a saint were subjected to a company of thieves, in due course the saint may become a thief.

People who are on a similar wavelength, apart from experiencing a natural attraction mentally or physically or both, will tend to go out of their way to help one another; on the other hand, we may reject others whose temperament and motivations we do not understand, because they are not on our wavelength. Compatibility becomes even more of a factor when we grow older, as parents try to influence their children's choice of profession or mate. All too often parents try to realize their own dreams through their children. We wish to see them become successful doctors, lawyers or businessmen if we ourselves found those to be rewarding and financially secure careers or, if we didn't get to try those professions and wished that we could have; or we want to see them do better in life than we did and try to protect them from the mistakes we made.

What happens if we are in disharmony with a brother or sister? Depending on how serious the disharmony is, it may lead to arguments or even fights. Choosing wrong or false friends can lead us to do things that can land us in trouble, while compatible friends will try to shield us and support us, when needed. A boss who understands and values us will try to help us move ahead, while another, who does not like us or our work may hinder our career or even fire us because we take a different approach.

Harmony in personal relationships is of paramount importance. A relationship can become a nightmare, once the physical attraction has worn off and the partners start to disagree on money or other matters, like how best to raise the kids. A truly successful personal relationship requires compatibility on the physical and mental levels, as well as tolerance for each other's religious or spiritual values. After all, most of our time is spent together on mundane matters like attending to basic needs of life and not in making love.

People who are mismatched can make each other's life hell. To give you an example, if a person born between March 22 and April 20 (Aries) is married to someone born between December 23 and January 20 (Capricorn), each will have a very different set of values, and hence they will not be able to agree on main issues of life like family life, politics or religion. Sometimes, one will become too dictatorial and overbearing, leaving no room for the other's beliefs or disagreements.

Carter's Orbital Puzzle

In the case of President Carter (see figure 12), we see a picture of very different vibrations creating great disharmony.

Three points to remember: 1. It is difficult to get a high position, 2. It is even harder to maintain the position acquired with much sweat and many tears, and 3. It is hardest to be able to use that high office to carry out all the improvements within the administration of the communities and country at large.

Jimmy Carter's horoscope is that of a gentle person with little resistance to any kind of opposition, one who is fond of peace and tranquility

Figure 12
The Orbital Puzzle of Pres. Jimmy Carter

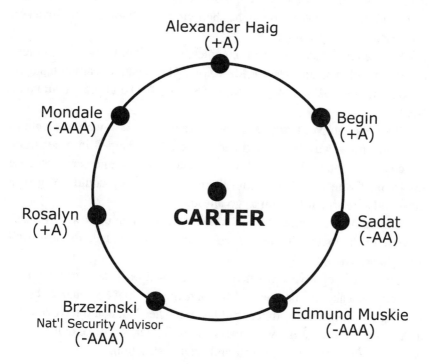

Alexander Haig
(+A)

Mondale
(-AAA)

Begin
(+A)

Rosalyn
(+A)

CARTER

Sadat
(-AA)

Brzezinski
Nat'l Security Advisor
(-AAA)

Edmund Muskie
(-AAA)

of mind and his environment.

It indicates great potentialities on intellectual levels, but lacks enough agility to enable him to forcefully implement any unpopular changes desired by him.

His is not the horoscope of a king, because the focus of his energies is rather distorted, which neutralizes the positive forces, thereby weakening the good effects of his moral and intellectual fiber.

The three positive people in his orbit, on a personal, professional and practical level were (Rosalyn [his wife +A], Alexander Haig [his Secretary of State +A] and Menachem Begin [+A], then Prime Minister of Israel, and one of the principal players responsible for the Middle East

Peace Treaty, but all three did not have a potent vibration cumulatively sufficient to effect any meaningful positive influence on President Carter. All three positives (+) mentioned have conflicting vibrations between themselves as individuals; hence, most of their energies neutralized each other and did not amount to much. Their individual vibrational impact on Mr. Carter was negligible.

It is better to have powerful enemies, rather than weaklings as close friends, which was the case for Mr. Carter. The negative team in his orbit were Edmund Muskie (-AAA), Anwar Sadat (-AA) and Walter Mondale (-AAA).

Even though Mr. Carter's friends meant well, they were not able to help him in the way he wanted and needed to be helped in order to be effective, partly because of Carter's own inadequacies, and partly because his friends were not clear within themselves, so they could not give a clear and sure signal for him to go ahead.

Sometimes our greatest harm comes to us through our own "friends" because of their stupidity, ignorance or lack of knowledge. To mean well alone is not enough.

The most negative influence was exercised on President Carter by one of his cabinet members, Mr. Brzezinsky, his National Security Adviser (-AAA) whose advice, if it had been heeded, could have led to a disastrous confrontation with the former Soviet Union engulfing the world community in nuclear war and final destruction.

President Carter could not be helped, even by his own friends, because he lacked the push and the mental force—so-called "charisma"—a factor marking individuals who are at once responsible for very brave deeds and who follow a path that the most daring would fear to tread.

Partnerships in business and politics between people who are incompatible can lead to business failures because of disagreements, and conflicts among cabinet members in an administration can lead to war due to unsound advice.

President Carter was surrounded by several people who had a disastrous influence on him. Begin and Sadat proved disastrous to him as president, and the negative vibrational impact on Carter impaired his own judgement in strategic national and international policy matters of great import, which eventually led to, and contributed to, his losing the election for a second term. In contrast to this, look at the orbital puzzle of

President Bill Clinton (see figure 13).

President Clinton is unique in modern history. His friends will be quite willing to help him and bail him out, despite all the wrangling and opposition from the most powerful Republican politicians, while totally ignoring ups and downs in the popular opinion.

There are three reasons why people help:

1. If a person is very powerful, others tend to help because of fear
2. If the person is loved to the point of worship
3. If the person is very popular because he or she may have espoused the public good.

Mr. Clinton has a very powerful vibration, which makes his magnetism very hard to resist.

Clinton's Orbital Puzzle

The illustration shows harmony (+A) or disharmony (-A) between Mr. Clinton and each person in his orbit. +AAA stands for maximum harmony, while -AAA means minimum harmony. The asterisk before a name means a karmic relationship from some past time, immediate or distant, implying scores to be settled with Mr. Clinton. The ellipses (between Bill and Hillary) show the vibrational exchange between these two people when they are within proximity of the aura ranges.

Bill Clinton has the horoscope of a king. He has the potentialities—physical, mental, and spiritual—to be able to rule large masses of people. This gives him a high rate of vibration (which is very uncommon), so that he is able to combat and overcome any hurdle or opposition with great ease, through the force of his will.

There are two key points to understand. He does and will attract powerful personalities to himself by virtue of his aura, which is potent, and has a great magnetic force that is hard to subdue or resist. Also, because of his personal magnetism, most people of a lower vibration will be hypnotized and drawn to him. Just as the sun eclipses all other bright objects, in the same way less bright or less powerful people who may try to steal his glory will be singed or overcome by his vibration.

Hillary, Al Gore and Vernon Jordan were three pillars that empowered Clinton, with enough mental and spiritual force by virtue of their strong vibrations so that his soul was fanned enough to perform at its best, and have

Figure 13
The Orbital Puzzle of Pres. Bill Clinton

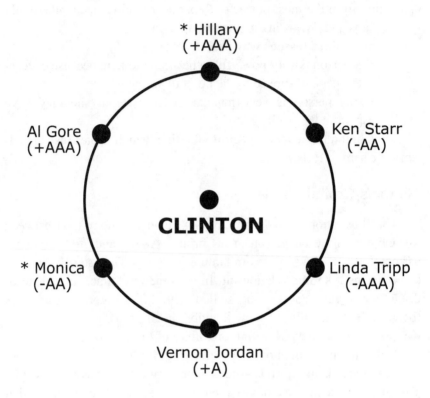

the power and energy to overcome the greatest difficulties with ease.

It means that even though he has Monica (-AA), Ken Starr (-AA) and Linda Tripp (-AAA) in his orbit, the total negative vibration produced by all these people is not sufficient to harm Clinton. Since all three have a nuisance value, Clinton's presidency will be blemished in history, just as Rasputin's negative influence left a mark on the Romanoff dynasty because of his bad influence, his nefarious activities, and his nuisance value.

How I was able to grade the nativities in the diagram above, I am not free to divulge. Suffice it to say that astrological and kabbalistic lores were the main contributory factors in the cumbersome process of such an analysis.

The Mystery of the Spotlight

The spotlight on an actor on the stage directs viewers' attention for as long as the light falls on him. On life's stage the good cycles of planets bring the person concerned into focus and suddenly that person comes into prominence—for the duration of the cycle. No sooner has the cycle ceased, than the same person becomes unimportant and soon forgotten. O. J. Simpson had a lot of spotlight placed upon him, but only as long as the court battles lasted, and now has been mostly forgotten. Such is the law of spotlights, which proves how fickle fate can be. To become obsolete is natural.

The positive results of the spotlight are as follows: The people surrounding this person in the spotlight, whether in the immediate vicinity or at a distance, will find him or her very attractive, and all the good adjectives will soon be attached to this person. His or her impact will be noticed in all areas of life, like business, social, personal affairs, or any other department. People will do all kinds of favors, will be helpful, courteous and will be quite willing and inspired to help materialize his or her dreams, aims or missions by cooperating financially, making right contacts for the person, even going as far as to secure a loan, and providing moral and social support.

All this will happen during the life of the positive cycle, because of the spotlight. This will bring unforeseen and unexpected opportunities into the life of the person concerned. Some other features will be increased, such as peace and harmony, within and around that person. The person will act maturely, and tactfully. Most endeavors will lead to positive results because most of the obstacles will be absent and more cooperation from colleagues will be forthcoming without anyone's asking for it. Writings and legal matters will succeed materially and satisfactorily. New ideas will be developed and pursued. Great mental stimulation will be in evidence and interesting experiences had. Family status will improve and the stocks held shall rise. New opportunities for personal advancement will present themselves and old dreams will materialize, honors and recognition will be received.

But not everyone comes under such a spotlight. Most people live and die in obscurity, their great talents neither recognized nor used for the public good. These people have a quiet nature and seek no publicity.

A Spotlight May Be Positive or Negative

The negative spotlight will be responsible for other conditions: Temporary overconfidence that may lead to unwise acts; there may be an inclination to be sarcastic, irritable, nervous and tense, showing a lack of patience and diplomacy; he or she may disregard established customs and traditions; and inner or outwardly expressed over-expectations may lead to disappointments and hurt feelings in friends and family. Tragedies may be constructed out of vague imaginings and plans for pleasure are apt to go wrong. The person will have less charm and not look so attractive because of a shrunken aura. He or she will count on the wrong person for a favor, someone who will be inclined to help an adversary. We will not be the center of attraction. Old wounds will open up, causing much grief.

Wise people seek good counsel as to the future, from an enlightened person, and prepare well in advance to use the positive spotlight or overcome the effects of the negative one. This technique of advance preparation can help one to benefit from the positive or go through the negative with less damage socially, materially and personally.

A good example of being caught in the negative spotlight is what happened to the great Irish poet, wit and playwright Oscar Wilde, when he brought a libel suit against John Sholto Douglas, ninth Marquess of Queensberry. Shortly afterwards, the Marquess countersued Mr. Wilde, charging him with indecent practices. There were three trials in all, lasting several years.

As a result of the negative spotlight, all of Wilde's weaknesses and vices were brought to light in the press, to the horror of his friends and members of his elite family. Until that time he was shining like a meteor, and had just successfully produced his play, *A Woman of No Importance*, in London. But there were some very inharmonious people in his orbit. Under the negative spotlight, he was discredited, publicly insulted, and actually even spat on. Fate had abandoned its favorite son, and now was the payback time. In May 1895, Mr. Wilde was sentenced to two years' hard labor. Upon his release from Pentonville prison in 1897, he went to France, where he died in exile at the age of forty-six.

Oscar Wilde's horoscope clearly warns against legal tangles and unfair publicity. This was fully corroborated by all the events that followed and the humiliation to which he was subjected. Such is the power of a negative spotlight. But not all those who lose the battle have a spotlight placed upon them, for as they say, "Many a flower blushes unseen."

One example of a positive spotlight is that of Ted Turner, who pledged $1 billion to the United Nations. Ted Turner is married to actress Jane Fonda, and owns cable TV stations, including TBS, TNT and others. He is considered a broadcasting giant, and has successfully launched a cable TV-station network around the globe. He happens to be that rare individual who, apart from being very wealthy, is very humane and believes in alleviating human suffering by financially supporting human-itarian enterprises wherever possible. Not all rich people have this kind of understanding of human suffering, once they have acquired wealth. Only those that are elevated spiritually show concerns about the welfare of those who are less fortunate.

Forewarned is forearmed. This information herewith presented, is in a condensed form; it is not meant to be complete, but is mentioned merely to indicate a contrast between the two. A spotlight may be positive or negative, depending upon the cycle. While a positive cycle will bring good, a negative cycle can ruin the person's life completely. Mind you, some people have a great staying power when faced with a calamity, while others don't last long enough even to physically survive a negative cycle.

To be oblivious of people in your orbit is a serious mistake and can lead to very extreme conditions in life. It must be borne in mind that no one person can perform all the roles in our lives satisfactorily and that's why we need the help of so many people to be successful in various departments of life. A person may be a fantastic mate but a total failure as a business partner.

The more people we have in our orbits who harmonize with us, the greater is the degree of our success, depending upon the plane of harmony. A perfectly harmonious vibration between two people, on a spiritual plane, is a most splendid thing and can lead to a state of bliss. So, friends, beware of these facts, and watch carefully who surrounds you.

There are certain people who carry with them a cataclysmic vibration. Either these people are attracted to the center of an event or to the zone of influence, or are the cause of it. They seem to attract a positive or negative event, like a peace treaty or an explosion, or to act as catalysts. It is my hypothetical assumption that there were three kinds of people aboard the *Titanic*:

- Those who had cataclysmic orbits in operation
- People with similar negative orbital vibrations
- Those who had preservative orbits.

You can guess which people perished and which survived.

Affirmation

I was made in the image of Almighty God, and hence I carry His spark. I have the right to be successful, happy and prosperous!

Questions and Answers

Q: *How do we know whether a person's influence is beneficial or not?*

A: The question you have posed is rather complicated because of the fact that some people appear to be very sweet without actually being good internally. The influence of people surrounding us is of different types and affects us on various levels, including the physical. Most of us are not aware of this. I will try to make it as simple as possible.

There are people who enter our orbit temporarily and leave an indelible mark on our character and destiny, in a negative or positive way, depending upon the vibrational exchange, for a long time to come. Another class of people stay in our orbit for a considerable period and yet do not deeply influence us one way or the other.

It takes a very deep study and analysis to really know the type of influence exercised by every person in our orbit at various times of our lives. This happens to be one of the mysteries of nature. But there are certain things we can learn and do.

It is possible to make horoscopes of all people in your orbit, and find out by comparison how each person influences the person concerned physically and mentally. If the astrologer is competent, the results will be sufficiently reliable. The more people we have around us who have a positive influence and bring a harmonious vibration, the greater will be the degree of our happiness and prosperity. To judge by how one feels in a person's company is utterly unreliable because it is possible to make a person feel good merely by thoughts. Feelings are most illusive.

Every person defines "beneficial" differently. Some judge things on a mundane level only. All such people remain oblivious of the two most important facets of life, the mental and spiritual, most essential for the salvation of a soul. The most important and congenial people are those who harmonize with us mentally and spiritually.

Q: *Is there a way to find out who will help us advance professionally?*

A: I know no easy answer to your question. We can try to anticipate who is going to be the next boss if we keep track of office politics, and if our relationship with the boss is reasonably good then professional advance should be fairly easy. There is another group of people who appear or disappear on or from the scene unexpectedly. It is very difficult to predict these, but there is one way. If we can find out who likes us and who doesn't, this will help us determine who will help or hinder our professional advancement.

Wherever there is harmony between two people, they normally help each other realize their goals. When we harmonize with a person we begin to feel comfortable with that person; this means attraction and a liking and we try to help those we like. It is only natural.

Q: *I have heard people say that as a couple, they had their charts compared by an astrologer. Do you think that it really helps?*

A: It can be of invaluable help to both the parties concerned provided it is done correctly by a competent astrologer. I stress the word "competent" because otherwise it will serve no useful purpose. A partner comparison indicates with unfailing accuracy the positive and negative aspects of personalities concerned, the degree of harmony or disharmony and where their interests will clash, whether or not they are likely to help each other, and locate the presence or absence of complementary qualities that are essential for success and mental stimulation.

Two people may do wonderfully well in bed but may be the worst of partners in business; there is always a life outside the bed, sometimes of greater importance. When two people are in mental harmony, they will tolerate each other's discrepancies and will be more cooperative and may even ignore any physical disharmony that may exist, because the mind is greater than the body. We have a double standard: one for those we harmonize with, and the other for those we don't.

Q: Can we block out negative influences from others?

A: In some cases it is possible, because since birth we are surrounded by people and we don't know most of the time who is negative. In cases where we have very few friends, getting rid of those would mean loneliness. But sometimes a choice has to be made between keeping the wrong company (company with the wrong vibrations) or loneliness. In my opinion it is better to be alone, rather than accept negative company. All that pleases is not always good for us. The penalty of wrong company can lead to a lowered sense of self-esteem and failure of all plans. It is better to take a long range view and stay in the right company, rather than enjoying a person who may, consciously or unconsciously, induce negative thoughts and thereby harm you. It is always wise to avoid negative company.

Q: When you say that people surrounding us can break us, do you mean only materially?

A: It is easier to notice things on a material level, since we are mostly not on a super -conscious level. It is a fact that we are very much influenced by the people who surround us. Their electro-magnetism can be a source of great inspiration or it can play havoc upon our mental state and impair our clear judgment. Whenever we come close to a person, we feel attraction or repulsion instantly. Most of us reject this feeling in favor of what the benefits of that company will be materially, but the repercussions will be serious if we ignore the warnings given by our feelings.

On a higher level, a wrong person can have a disastrous influence on the ruler of a nation and then the entire country will suffer. This has happened in many cases in history. Rasputin had a negative influence on the Czar of Russia and an empire came to an end. We should never underestimate what kind of influence our friends have on us.

The most important single ingredient in the formula of success is the knack of getting along with people.

—THEODORE ROOSEVELT

The Star Guide
for Businessmen

Business is like riding a bicycle.
Either you keep moving or you fall down.

—JOHN DAVID WRIGHT

Some people are born with money sense and some acquire it by training. The lucky ones who have the knack of multiplying money, make all the right choices in their investments and become wealthy in a much shorter time than the rest.

It does not matter how much you make, it is how much you keep that matters.

It is correct to say that money does not exist. It is merely a concept, a means of exchange that replaces the barter system. Because our social, political and economic climate changes constantly, a very conservative outlook is required in order to survive a financial catastrophe, should our leaders mess up.

Financial security is a myth. It, too, does not exist. Because our money loses its purchasing power constantly, we do not really make money even though we seem to on paper. The rate of inflation and the interest rate are two other factors that can eat into our savings.

Americans generally do not save as much as the Japanese and the Western Europeans. We live on credit and hence any negative social event like a divorce, separation or a terminal disease can wipe out the finances of an entire family. We must start saving at an early age, keeping in view our entire life span, and allowing for any untoward incidents. Financial provision must be made and sufficient money must be available to face any tragedies, so that we can survive.

Money provides two things, freedom and financial independence.

In itself, it is nothing but energy; it opens doors to great opportunities if correctly used. If used incorrectly, it can do irreparable harm.

In the Western hemisphere, we judge a person by the amount of money or wealth he or she apparently has. Money management requires a great expertise—not only the money sense, but also the vision to forsee coming changes and movements in the financial climate of the country where we invest.

Successful investment advisors possess an understanding of current events and a vision of future events, social and political, and their impact on the economies of the world. Any miscalculation in this regard can lead to large financial losses. This is exactly what happened in the nineties to those who invested big in emerging markets. They failed to see that the patterns of society were changing and moving toward sharp restrictions, imposed as a result of the philosophical changes in those nations toward foreign investors. Under such a restrictive environment, free enterprise succumbs and the investors incur large scale losses.

Money management and wealth-building can be learned by studying financial newspapers. The need for wealth-building depends upon our family's needs and lifestyle. A working family of four will have very different financial needs from the family of an independent businessman who trades internationally.

What does money buy? All material things. What does it not buy? Happiness, love, peace, good health, spiritual evolution and nirvana and an extension of our life span, or intellectual growth and expansion. Money can solve most problems. It can also create many problems and complications. Some people kill for it.

Optimally, every person should have at least two sources of income—earnings and investments—and a reserve fund for unforeseen emergencies.

Money Management

Money management requires a great expertise. If you are not good at it, invest only in most conservative businesses based on tested and tried methods. You will have a lesser return in terms of money, but your money will be reasonably secure and you will have peace of mind.

But, remember: Nothing is perfectly safe. A buggy-whip company with a long history of paying big dividends was a good investment in 1800. By 1850, it paid less and had a less rosy future. Today, of course, that company isn't even in existence. The economy of a country depends upon various factors that are beyond our control, such as the ever-shifting global political, economic and social elements. The emerging markets have had a great impact on all investments and they affect individual countries in the economic sense.

All those who choose the most conservative investments have more peace of mind, even if the stock market suddenly tumbles. Higher risk investments are by definition more uncertain and require the investor to be seasoned and thick-skinned. If you are a sensitive type, pay some reliable and established company to manage your money and invest it in conservative enterprises like utilities, government bonds and triple A stocks alone. About 40 percent must be kept liquid to create a breathing space, just in case.

When planning your financial future, consider your age, energy level and general health. Also consider the zone you are in: A, B or C (high energy, medium or low).

Most people will need to engage a reputable and established investment advisor and financial planner to cope with the fast-changing nature of today's world economies, where the safety of invested capital is of prime concern to all investors, especially people of limited means.

Cash will be king in the twenty-first century because of the credit economies that are fast approaching. Plan your finances, including some form of insurance for the short term (two years), midterm (five to ten years), and long term (ten to fifteen years). This maneuver will save you many a heartache, should the politicians mess up and the emerging markets swallow your invested capital. Bear in mind:

- Everything is not written in stone. This means we can undo what we have done in the past. And that is where free will comes in.
- We are all on this planet to change for the better, to learn, improve and evolve.
- To say: "What will be, will be" is fatalistic. That statement is not in keeping with the natural laws.
- Check your plans for the future against figure 7, page 46, to be sure you factor your own energy level (and/or other family

members) into what you are planning, both to have and to do, for yourself and others.

- God gave us each freedom of thought and action, and we must exercise both for self-improvement.
- No one else can make decisions for us. It is our right, and privilege, to make the right decisions to suit our purpose. And we must be prepared to pay for our mistakes or blunders in coin or kind.
- Astrology is a torch that shows (if the astrologer is competent) the pitfalls and opportunities as they appear on the path of life. It must be used intelligently and wisely to improve our lot in life.

I do not believe in any magic wand someone can wave to change our conditions overnight. I firmly believe in logic, science, hard work and long-term personal concerted efforts. I am very skeptical of those who profess to bring back the dead. I provide the best information possible to my client based on a correctly constructed chart and explain the courses open to him or her. But the client has to make the decisions and be responsible for them. Life is a battle, we win some and lose some.

If I were to say, "This is going to happen, according to the stars," I imply that unless you do something to change the course of your life, this is the pattern likely to emerge. I don't believe in any fanatical, fatalistic nonsense. I firmly believe in the independence and dignity of every soul incarnated on earth, each of which is unique. Reason, logic, practicality, an open mind and willingness to change for the better is what I practice and believe. There are no quick fixes in life. It is a long and cumbersome process to correct the mistakes of the past, whether of our own making or others'.

Aries (March 22 to April 20)

Though you possess a great capacity for making money, you tend to be extravagant at times. Where money management of others is concerned, your decisions will not always depend upon much reflection, but rather rash actions. This can cause financial turmoil and great losses in a negative cycle when your judgement is likely to be greatly hampered. Owing to the very desire to attempt large transactions, you will, at times, incur heavy losses and fluctuations of financial fortunes.

Even though you will be very determined to acquire wealth, only very judicious investments will prove most beneficial.

Your most positive traits are a great organizing ability in a business, but you are very independent; you must have things done your own way. Very frank and outspoken, you lack caution and react to a situation without much reflection, which can cause you much financial loss at times. Your greatest positive trait is an abundance of courage.

What you should avoid: Flattery usually clouds your judgment, and arrogant reactions can cause huge financial losses and failure of plans. Aries natives can be brutal and tyrannical. They have little patience in any undertaking and seek quick results. For this reason all pursuits requiring long labor and much reflection are unsuitable for you.

You should invest in: Political organizations, large and prestigious clubs, international organizations, army and navy, ammunition factories, tank building companies, railroads and railroad building materials.

Pitfalls to avoid: Even though you possess a great earning capability and moral courage and endurance, you are prone to large and extravagant ideas financially. Should any of your projects be commenced in a negative cycle, non-conducive to financial success, you are likely to lose most of your investment. Because you are very conscientious and practical, you will be most suited to managing other people's money, but any tendency to lavish action must be controlled to avoid very sudden heavy losses.

Taurus (April 21 to May 21)

Generally speaking, you will be lucky in financial matters. You will gain through partnerships with individuals and organizations. You will be interested in opening things up, development of lands, mines and minerals and profitable exploitation of them. Equally favorable for you will be property management, and building projects like hotels and restaurants.

You should invest in: Mining, agriculture, forestry, paper pulp, real estate, building materials, building construction (homes and business complexes), music (CD) manufacturing, and the singing business in general.

Pitfalls to avoid: You will easily come into money but for the preservation of your capital, you will need the help of a financial planner. Generally speaking, you should avoid speculative investments like banking institutions and insurance companies, even though they may offer good returns, and remain content with a smaller, safer return.

Gemini (May 22 to June 21)

Since you have a sharp brain, most of the laborious ventures will be disagreeable to you. You tend to want to make money quickly.

Investments of a speculative nature will be most appealing to you. The stock market will have a special fascination for you. No matter how successful you may become financially, you will always crave more. When you take greater risks to gratify these desires, you may overreach yourself. Overwork in this area could lead to a cessation of effort and financial uncertainty as a consequence.

You should invest in: Banking industry, financial institutions, insurance companies, law firms, speakers' bureaus, art, and the entertainment industry generally.

Pitfalls to avoid: Your keen intellect will help you make money very easily, but you should weigh and balance the risk factors and the nervous energy involved in all your investments in your bid to get rich quickly. You have a good intuition about speculation, but you can get carried away by your impatience which can cost you plenty. Try to be satisfied with a reasonable gain rather than the prospects of big money with a very high risk and hidden costs in nervous strength. Risk only as much as you can handle so that you don't overreach yourself.

Cancer (June 22 to July 23)

Because of your sensitive nature and the tendency to trust others, you should beware of fraudulent people disguised as sympathizers. Scrutinize well all the companies and syndicates that offer huge returns for a small outlay, before investing your own money. In all your financial dealings, be extremely careful and cautious before signing any legal contracts, agreements and documents, even if the risk factor appears to be very little.

You should invest in: Oil or coal, shipping companies that are well-established, in radium, platinum, electric power concerns, antiques, curios, drug companies, liquor enterprises and public utilities.

Pitfalls to avoid: Other people's dishonorable intentions may result in your financial losses. Beware of all syndicates and fraudulent companies that offer you a large return on your small investment. You should exercise extreme caution in all money matters, carefully avoiding any agreements and contracts with the slightest element of risk or uncertainty. Money will come to you in very peculiar ways at times when you least expect it. It is the future security of your finances you should most worry about.

Leo (July 24 to August 23)

Investments in most legitimate businesses will prove beneficial. Speculative ventures will bring you money generally. Judicious investing on a large scale in a public concern will be a favorable area.

You should invest in: Gold mining, brass products, diamond mining, municipals of all kinds, the import and export of provisions involving foreign governments, are all areas where you may expect good returns on your investments.

Pitfalls to avoid: In a general way you will get more financial breaks than most people. Legitimate businesses and enterprises will prove most rewarding. You will make killings on the stock market as a result of your hunches, and through judicious investments in public companies. You tend to invest on a large scale taking huge risks. You should beware of diplomatic and slick salesmen who may try to prey upon your generosity.

Virgo (August 24 to September 23)

You possess a good business sense and a careful, frugal nature.

You should invest in: You will be lucky in land deals, mining, paper pulp, paper manufacturing companies, forestry, land development and real estate in general.

Pitfalls to avoid: You are endowed with a good business sense. You will be lucky in creating large businesses or industries. Financial successes will come to you as a result of your brain power but you will tend to be over-anxious about your future and try more than one avenue to make money. You should carefully scrutinize any wills or contracts presented to you because an oversight of any flaws would prove quite costly to you. Your future security should be carefully planned.

Libra (September 24 to October 23)

You have a scientific way of looking at things and would like a reason why an investment should be made. You can amass great wealth, if you can convince yourself that you should. Your higher sense of values will not allow you to make money at any cost, especially if it would mean compromising your principles. Your capacity to save will be rather hampered because of your faith in the cosmic laws. You could easily train yourself in the financial field (money management and investments). By doing so, your desire to live with dignity will be gratified.

You should invest in: Jewelry (Eastern and Western), paintings, brokerage houses, banking institutions, money management outfits, engineering companies, architectural enterprises, electric generating plants and artist's materials.

Pitfalls to avoid: You are blessed with a remarkable brain and your idealistic dreams could be easily transmuted into great financial gains for you, provided you are assisted by a successful money manager who is trained in tackling financial situations of any type and a financial planner. Do not try to manage your own money. Leave that to the experts.

Scorpio (October 24 to November 22)

Being very receptive to outward stimuli, you can be easily duped by designing characters and con artists, who will be out to fleece you. Because of these reasons, you will experience many ups and downs in your financial fortunes. You tend to be over generous and lavish in spending. You could easily fall a prey to any demands made on your generosity for financial help in adversity, especially from members of the opposite sex. It is strongly advised that you engage an investment adviser to plan your financial future.

You should invest in: Musicals (in films, on TV, and on the stage) and music production companies, drug manufacturing, dentists' materials, and mechanical engineering firms and machinery.

Pitfalls to avoid: You can be easily persuaded into joining any financial scheme even if it lacks a solid foundation. You tend to be very trusting and perhaps too optimistic. You should keep your expenses well under control, and save a part of what you make. Carefully invest in solid enterprises. You should make a long-term financial plan as early as possible to secure your future; if not, your advancing years could prove very difficult materially.

Sagittarius (November 23 to December 22)

Your luck factor being very high, you will have more than the usual number of opportunities to make money, through your own work or your mental prowess. You will be better off following your own intuitions, most of the time. Take no partners.

You should invest in: Research lab products, financial institutions, savings and loan, banking industry, financial management, and insurance companies.

Pitfalls to avoid: You will be quite lucky in all money matters provided you stick to your own intuition. Should you follow any stock market "tips" you will incur heavy losses. You will be better off remaining a lone wolf. Any financial partnership will prove a big mistake and a liability. You can expect to gain through a legacy but be wise to carefully invest the proceeds. You will have to constantly guard against high expenses so that you may live with dignity in later years.

Capricorn (December 23 to January 20)

Because of delays, hindrances and limiting circumstances in your life, any money made will have to be earned. You will be forced to economize and be thrifty, but that is something you are good at naturally.

You should invest in: Manufacturing, wholesale clothing, building materials, real estate development, mining, agriculture products, forestry, timber, wood pulp, paper manufacturing, building up factories, and lead or iron products.

Pitfalls to avoid: You will make money by overcoming many difficulties, and everything (huge losses or gains) in your financial fortune will go to extremes. You can expect a windfall in the form of an inheritance. You should avoid lending money without security or you may lose it. Do not lend on speculation.

Aquarius (January 21 to Febuary 19)

The most unexpected happenings in your life, generally, will not permit you to plan your finances to a great degree. You will be wise to engage a financial planner to secure your material future, and to keep your humane and humanitarian urges well under control. Make it a habit to save at least ten percent of what you make every month.

You should invest in: Research projects involving the human psyche, banking industry, brokerage houses, public speaking enterprises, educational institutions and organizations, invention merchandising, architectural products, trusts, insurance companies, electrical installations, and aviation.

Pitfalls to avoid: You are likely to come across people who will make a demand on your money by playing upon the humanitarian side of your nature. Do not gamble with other people's financial interests or you will wind up paying from your own pocket. Try to bite off only what you can chew, otherwise your money matters will get out of your control. To preserve your personal capital, someone else should manage your money.

Pisces (February 20 to March 21)

You would want to be rich, but this desire will have to be backed by persistent efforts to get results. You will have your share of crosses to bear. You need to train yourself to pursue your financial projects to a successful conclusion. More concentration of mind will be imperative, if your finances have to be secure for the advancing years. You will badly need a financial planner to create a workable plan, and you must stick to it.

You should invest in: Manufacturing concerns, steamship companies (both cargo and luxury liners), waterways, import and export by sea, organizations engaged in humanitarian research (on diseases like cancer, muscular dystrophy, or Alzheimer's), educational institutions, public speaking bureaus, dance institutions, drama and theater outfits.

Pitfalls to avoid: You will have dreams of building a financial fortune but may lack the traits to control it and the physical effort to attain it. By training, you could easily learn the techniques of money-making, and you have the persistence required. Your careless or indifferent attitude to money matters will be a major stumbling block, and it would require a drastic change in order to succeed in material matters. Because of the ups and downs in your financial future, you would be wise to employ a money manager and stay on the safe side.

Questions and Answers

Q: The stock market moves in cycles. What governs the ups and downs of the market?

A: As an investment adviser and editor of *Ostaro's Market Newsletter*, I have a particular view on this subject. Here, I am going to talk only on a global level. In the international aspect, various factors determine any particular direction the stock market in any country takes. These factors are the geopolitical situation, (meaning the degree of peace and political stability of a nation), the general health of its national economy, its foreign obligations (i.e. the foreign debt to be repaid), its gross national product, the degree to which it depends upon other nations for its economic and political survival, and the state of its national security.

These are only some of the factors. We must also consider how the rest of the industrialized world is going to grow. For instance, if the immediate future of the world economy looks bleak, without any prospect of sustained industrial growth, the stock market can only remain bullish for a while. We have to remember that the market is comprised of both bulls and bears at all times, and any drastic or assumed change in the political or economic state of a country will directly impact all the investors, for better or worse.

The stock market fluctuates because of the emotional state of people or any kind of commotion on a local, national or international level. Technical and fundamental factors alone cannot predict the health of any economy. The public reaction is an emotional reaction to any event, and it instantly translates into a market fluctuation. Should there be uncertainty about the consequences of such an event, which may have long-term repercussions socially or economically on a national level, then the trend will continue as long as the emotional state persists.

For example, if the peace in the Middle East is threatened, this will have a direct impact on all the oil consuming countries, threatening their oil supply, and oil prices will tend to go up. The opposite is also true; if Middle East peace were to be achieved, one could expect oil prices slowly to move downwards, as no scarcity is likely.

An event is only partly responsible for market ups and downs. What really triggers mass buying and selling is how nervous people feel about their own future. Whenever our future security or prosperity is threatened, we react or over-react to an event. Many investors, in a state of high emotion, lose their shirts by selling out too soon, because they lack staying power, and jitters are highly contagious. It is usually wise to take the long-term view and let the things simmer down before making a move, provided our survival is not at stake.

Affirmation

I shall have by _____ an earned income of _____, an invested income of _____ per month, and a reserve fund for emergencies of ten percent of my total income by _____. I pledge to secure my financial future, so that having done that I can focus on my spiritual well-being, my sole purpose for being on this planet. Just as a hungry person only thinks of food, in the same manner a poor person is always occupied with ways of making money and life passes him by and his real soul-transforming work is ignored and never attended to.

> *When you lend money to a friend, you will*
> *lose both—the friend and the money.*
>
> —OSTARO

Focusing Your Energies For Success

The truest wisdom, in general, is resolute determination.

—NAPOLEON BONAPARTE

The energy focus diagrams (Figure 14 and 14A on the next page) illustrate how one's total energies, when properly directed to any one aim at a time, will successfully overcome all difficulties and lead to success, while forces scattered in more than one direction will not lead to any meaningful results.

In order to tap the total energy needed, we will have to make a demand from the energy reservoir. And then the requisite amount of energy will be released. Learning a technique of mental concentration is a must for this operation to be done right. The greater the power of concentration, the better the results will be.

Big projects, involving the destinies of thousands of people, require a very careful handling of the energy bank. The availability of energy will depend upon how many demands on it have already been made. One can run out of personal energy, just as smaller tanks, confronted with large demands, let one run out of hot water (in a house) or gas (in a car). Some energy banks can and do contain a lot more energy than others. It all depends upon the individuals.

Great personalities do not think of anything else except their object of immediate attention, until such time as energy has been fully utilized for the successful completion of the undertaking at hand. In case of any mishaps in the process, without such careful supervision, everything could go amiss and total failure would result.

Leaders in the political arena, who represent the fate of many thousands of people, have to steer clear of unnecessary obstructions, so the requisite amount of energy is used only for the success of the project at hand, carefully avoiding any unnecessary spending of energy. Any diversion of the ener-

Figure 14
Energy Focus

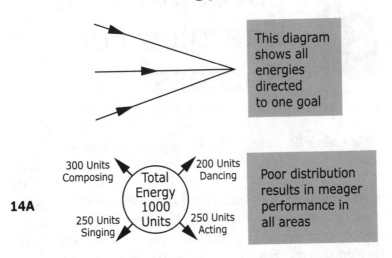

14A

This diagram shows all energies directed to one goal

300 Units Composing — Total Energy 1000 Units — 200 Units Dancing — 250 Units Singing — 250 Units Acting

Poor distribution results in meager performance in all areas

Figure 14: Figure 14A may be likened to the human energy reservoir with four taps. (See Fig. 5). If all four taps were open at the same time, the pressure (or intensity of energy) will be considerably reduced and may not turn the human turbine to desired action. In simple words, a task requiring 1000 units of energy may only get a portion of that amount, and the job will remain half done. For instance, water normally boils at 100 degrees centigrade; if we were to provide insufficient heat, the water would become lukewarm, but would not boil under normal pressure.

Hence we conclude that to reach a particular goal within a certain time period, maximum intensity of force is as essential as the force itself.

Intensity depends upon the pressure of circumstances we are under. For instance, if I decided to go on a cruise four days from today, I would be under tremendous pressure to take care of so many obligations (social and otherwise) like paying all the bills, boarding my pet, etc. I will be achieving much, (under the pressure of circumstances) taking care of many things within four days which would normally take me four times longer to achieve the same results. The pressure creates intensity, and intensity gets the job done fast.

Water boils on a mountain top but it won't cook anything for lack of atmospheric pressure. Moral: pressure of circumstances and intensity of force are the key factors in the measurement of human performance.

gy released will lead to tremendous waste and poor results. Efficient usage of the human energy reservoir is wisdom. Those who carelessly over-spend their substance in youth, are at a loss and do not have the sufficient amounts of energy in later years for even their most urgent needs. This situation makes them dependent upon those who have abundant energy (the youth). The problem is that our human body generates less and less energy as we grow older, because our system does not function as efficiently, so our immune system gets weaker and the energy bank gets depleted much quicker.

Let me clarify one point about efficiency. Only a part of the semen released from the body is used to fertilize the egg, and the rest is wasted—but it only takes one. The degree of efficiency at which one operates will largely determine the efficacy of energy usage. Towards this end, it is imperative that the mind, that has total control over energy release, be under control and most of the energy released be focused on overcoming the problems involved in the success process of a project.

It has been observed that great leaders in the past have so focused their minds (for good or evil) that they have been labeled fanatics, lunatics or maniacs. In all such cases, the *technique* used was adequate but the *intention* we deem unworthy. Energy of any kind, like electricity, is neither good nor bad in itself, and may be used to help thousands or be abused to annihilate millions.

When NASA decided to send a probe to the moon, a few points had to be most carefully calculated: the distance of the moon from the earth, the gravitational pull of the earth, and the thrust required to overcome the gravitational pull plus the energy needed to get the rocket to the moon and back, as well as the amount of time the entire mission would take. The rocket has to focus on the moon, and a slight variation in its course could send it thousands of miles off course, and away from the moon. In the same way— when we don't keep the object of our desire in full view and in focus, we could pass it by or never see it.

There are allied pursuits like dancing, playing guitar and miming. These belong to the same category of entertainment and they are not conflicting in nature. If you were to pursue all three of these at once, you are likely at least to become a Jack of all trades, a dilletante, dancing a little, miming a little and playing a few notes on the guitar—but you will not shine in any one.

Mediocrity pleases no one. Success and mastery in each will suffer as a result of split focus, but at least they don't force the mind to think in opposite directions. If I were to try to learn stock market analysis and film-making at the same time, this would divide my energies in opposite directions. Because we divide our focus, most of us are not masters of any particular art or science.

Excellence in any pursuit is achieved when all the three levels of our being (physical, mental and spiritual) are well coordinated and harmonious. This is the mark of a master. World personalities that I had the good fortune to study and analyze, all had this kind of coordination of their energies. I have studied the personalities of Presidents Nixon, Reagan, Carter and Clinton, Menachem Begin, Nehru, Anwar El-Sadat, Hosni Mubarak and Mikhail Gorbachev, as well as Napoleon, The Duke of Wellington and Queen Victoria, just to name a few.

Energy conflict creates tension and that is what constitutes stress. The higher the tension, the greater the stress. Hypertension reduces the scope of the magnetic power we all possess. Our mental focus specially indicates where our energies are being focused. It is futile and very wasteful to create tension within the self. Especially when we learn that by focusing, we can avoid splitting our energies and creating unnecessary inner conflicts. Yes, we should live to our fullest potential. But most of us don't.

Generally speaking, we live on a thirty to forty percent energy range. Simply stated, we possess sixty to seventy percent more latent energy than we use. It is a grave blunder not to realize what we can do to improve our lot. The saying "Know thyself" has a deep meaning. It implies knowing our potential. What gods can do, we mortals can do too, did we but know it to be possible.

It is a serious mistake to underrate the limits to which we can stretch our potential. Some of our best traits are never used. Why? First, because we don't know that we have them, and secondly, because we are very uncomfortable with anything new, for it implies changing an old habit.

Over the centuries humanity has been told that where there is muck there is money. We feel guilty when we try to become rich, or even just a little bit less poor. We believe we have sinned—although I don't know against what or whom. I maintain that the Creator meant us to be happy, successful and prosperous.

One of the biggest battles in life is focusing our energies toward any one aim. From birth, we focus our energies on many different goals. This energy expenditure has to be more carefully planned than the spending of money, because we can make more money if we have the energy—but not vice versa.

Deciding to focus our energies to successfully complete a project from its conceptual stage to final success is a similar process. The conditions we are in have a certain pull on us. Wordsworth said, "The world is too much with us." We are like the silkworm in its cocoon. It seems hard to get out of the place we are in. We need a big push or a kick to overcome the conditions that bind us, enough energy to carry on, a specified direction or goals toward which to direct our energies, and then the release of requisite amounts of energy till the job is done. All this is good.

One key point to remember: Even if our energies are properly controlled and directed, most of them will still be wasted. For, without proper focus, no results may ensue.

If I had lunch with my bank manager, and I spent the time in talk about the quality of food served, making no effort to convince him why he should grant me the loan I am asking for, he is likely to think that I don't need the money very much and we're just having a social meeting.

What we want has to be made crystal clear; first, within our own mind and then to those with whom we do business, so that we provide the adequate signals to our super-conscious mind. We seem to make many tactical mistakes unconsciously, and then we assume, when things go wrong, that Lady Luck has just not favored us.

Think of a dam with an outlet controlling millions of gallons of water. As long as the outlet is closed, the water appears so calm and harmless and we see no signs of energy and power or pressure. In order to generate electric power, the outlet has to be opened and then the water will rush out with great force, having been carefully focused to make the turbine turn. The force or pressure of water turns the turbine, creating thousands of watts of electric power. This example illustrates the point: the water reservoir, the demand made for the release of water through a narrow outlet, and the resulting focus of the released water on the moving turbine.

As human beings, we have a similar system in operation. A human being contains tremendous amounts of energies, but we do need an outlet and a focus to do great deeds with our energies. It is not possible, to my knowledge, to measure the total energy we possess. The thought machines can measure only our force of mental concentration.

Let us imagine that we possess unlimited amounts of energy being funneled from the Great Source; we would still require great mental concentration for its release to open the outlet at the right time. Then there remains the question of focusing it on a particular project. If we have doubts about the total amounts of energy, as a result of a miscalculation or a bad self-image and a poor capability to concentrate, we will fail to tap the energy present in our system and the problem of focusing it on any project will never even arise. It is a great pity that so many people continue to live in an energy bankrupt environment on a conscious level, and hence make no demands upon their own energy system whatsoever.

Great men or women become aware of their potential from childhood and make many demands on their systems in a normal way, through a technique of mental concentration. They also apply that concentration to their lofty aims. Mahatma Gandhi, a barrister at law from Oxford, England, appeared to be a frail man, yet he possessed a powerful will and unceasing energy. He used this power and energy for the good of humanity. He used passive resistance against the British rule in India, and drove them out without engaging in an armed conflict, since he was a pacifist and a nonviolent man.

We each have to realize our own potential. The real key seems to be awareness of what we have, coupled with confidence about using it. A bank statement showing a large amount of money in an account confirms our belief that we have large funds available in exact and specific terms. The trouble is that assumptions about our untapped energy resources can't be so exact—they cannot be measured mathematically to give us surety and confidence in our powers. It pains me to observe that the human race has lived in partial or total ignorance of its potential for thousands of years.

A thought takes twenty seconds to travel from the brain to a piece of paper to be written, but it may take ten times longer to understand what we read. This conversion rate being so slow is quite baffling to me. It depends upon the nature of our constitution and our reflexes, not to mention our short attention span.

Interestingly, mental concentration can actually be measured by an apparatus for thought photography and register of cerebral forces invented by the French savant, Monsieur E. Savary d'Odiardi in the nineteenth century, according to Count Louis Hamon (Cheiro), the great sage and occultist of the twentieth century.

Those who are highly developed mentally and spiritually, normally have a very high rate of vibration and are endowed with higher faculties far more advanced than most people's. They comprehend more quickly and they better understand things on a mental plane. The coarser the vibration, the duller the person, mentally and physically. Some people have an I.Q. of 140 while others have to rest content with a meager 110. Coarser vibrations indicate impurities or toxins in the physical or ethereal or ideational body. In such cases the soul remains an unhappy prisoner. Very little spiritual advancement is made in a lifetime with a lot of extra baggage, in the form of accumulated karma, to be carried over into the next incarnation.

But there is always hope. We certainly can undo what we may have done wrong. I wish things were simpler in the patterns of creation. God has so arranged His or Her affairs that a mere realization of our limits is just the beginning in our bid for self-perfection and salvation. Souls are encased in bodies; they can't get out without dying. Or atttaining total transformation. For most material endeavors, we don't require as much physical and mental effort, comparatively speaking, as for our soul's total salvation.

But one thing stands out most vividly and clearly in my mind—it is the word "focus." Without focus, no results may be predicted for the future with any degree of certainty or precision.

In fact, without focus—no matter how great our supply of energy—we get terrible results. Because our efforts are not directed toward any ONE goal, we often get no results at all. What a waste!

What is your life's focus? Apart from making a living, do you have a hobby that you enjoy immensely? What is your greatest strength? Can you sell insurance, write a speech, deliver a lecture or fix a plumbing problem, run for political office and win? Can you sketch a flower or paint a sunset? Cook a good dinner or whistle a merry tune? What are *you* good at? What is it you seek most?

In order to focus our energies, we have to become aware of them. Some people have more physical prowess and others are intellectual giants, while a God-realized yogi possesses cosmic consciousness. We must take stock of our energies and then learn the art or technique of focusing them on any particular aim we have. Some people have the inborn faculty of concentrating all their forces upon what they are doing at any time, but others have to learn it through training and by practicing to totally channel their forces. Those who are involved in more than one project have scattered their energies and will most likely never excel in any of them.

Abraham Lincoln was one of the most ambitious human beings his friends had ever seen. He had an aspiration for a high station in life that burned in him like a furnace. He taught himself the law entirely by himself. He was literally a self-made lawyer. He entered the Illinois Legislature at the age of twenty-five. In the 1850s he was one of the most sought-after attorneys. He had put his focus on what mattered to him—so he got it.

The Success Puzzle

A most creative process of directing energy is governed by the law of duality of creation, which is not a figment of human imagination. This translates into a wonderful personality and superior traits that baffle normal reason and logic.

The energy generated by perseverance and determination can be compared to a charging bull kept in check by a trap door, to be released at the right moment. This force will, if used correctly, break the back of failure for good, and help the person concerned to accomplish his or her task quite satisfactorily.

Great souls have noble missions to fulfill, and are fanned by an indomitable will to combat all obstacles at all costs to reach the desired goal, but not in violation of any natural laws that must be observed. Constant work toward a well-defined goal, coupled with one-pointed attention and with a persistent attitude, perseverance and determination—these are the hallmarks of a Divine plan, and as such, will have to succeed eventually and will materialize the planner's goals on the physical plane.

We must realize that no one succeeds in any cause on his or her own. It is the combined effort of all the people involved in the project plus the forces of nature that make the whole thing work. The credit of success thus achieved must be given to all the forces. That includes the individual who caused the materialization of the project (whose mould was created by nature, unseen) on a physical plane.

No great task has ever been accomplished without concentration and focus of energies. In order to become a great actor, apart from being talented, we need to study acting techniques. We must decide whether we want to become a character actor or a comedian. If, instead of concentrating on becoming a character actor, we decide to study singing and dancing as well as acting, scattering our energies, we may end up with small mediocre roles instead of those that go to great actors.

A good example of concentration and focus is Thomas Edison, who invented the light bulb. He tried, literally, thousands of possible metals and designs for a possible filament, discarding each that failed until he discovered what did work. He focused his energy on each experiment until he achieved success.

We don't realize how often the forces in the unseen come to our rescue when we are faced with gigantic problems. We may boastfully take all the credit unto ourselves, ignoring those who contributed as much as we did. The potter is merely the cause who takes the temporary role of the Creator to mould clay into a priceless sculpture. From then on the sculpture begins to live.

If a project, of necessity, requires one thousand units of energy to successfully complete it, it will never be completed with only seven hundred units. It will always be three hundred units short. We must first mentally measure the energy requirement we need, then find ways to divert that much energy. Just as a weak and malnourished horse cannot pull a carriage with four passengers, a person lacking in will cannot successfully pull off a Herculean task without outside help.

Questions and Answers

Q: What happens if the energies of a person are scattered?

A: A person who attempts four things at once has mediocre results for want of focus, while the person who does only one can finish it and move to the next. Every project requires a certain amount of energy and a lack of the requisite amount never leads to success. Water boils at 100 degrees centigrade. If we don't supply enough heat, the water will become hot, but it will never boil.

Q: What can we do to acquire concentration?

A: I think you mean mental concentration. According to my studies, mind is the hardest thing to control. It requires many long hours of practice to control the mind through a breathing technique. Breath controls life; hence, it has great sway over the human mind. Once mind has become reasonably controlled, it becomes easier to concentrate it on anything. The most potent thing is concentrated thought acquired through a disciplined and balanced life.

Q: Is concentration an ability we are born with, or can it be acquired?

A: I believe that all of us have a certain amount of it. Some develop it through practice. The astrological lore reveals that certain signs of the Zodiac do possess great amounts of mental concentration. It happens to be one of the greatest boons of nature, for once we have sufficient degree of concentration of mind, every hurdle in life is easily overcome by fully applying all the forces we have, and success in every project comes quite easily.

If you find it hard to concentrate on anything, the best route to success would be to take a yoga course. It will help enormously; little by little you will be able to develop your concentration.

Q: *Apart from concentration, what else is required to be successful?*

A: You will also need a will to succeed and a strong determination. Both these are latent powers we all are blessed with in varying degrees. As long as we breathe we all have the will, but the strength of determination depends upon the constitution of every individual. Some people have physical strength par excellence, while others are intellectual giants, and there are still others whose energies are totally focused on the spiritual plane. Some others have all the three in varying degrees.

Will and determination are mental traits, both of which are essential to success, since they help the human reservoir release the energies needed. Only when we "will" does the tap open to release the energy. You will notice that in an emergency, you automatically will the energy to be released with full force, because all your mind is fully focused on just one thing.

Q: *To what extent does ambition contribute to our focus on a particular goal?*

A: There is an interrelationship of ambition and will. It is my considered opinion that those who have ambition do possess a strong will. Yes, it is possible to have a will but no ambition but it is rare.

Ambition impels a person to exercise will to a high degree, and his goal comes into focus automatically. Without ambition, I doubt very much whether a person will succeed in any noble aim, for, even if he possesses the necessary resources, he will not call them into play appropriately.

Seest thou a man diligent in his business?
He shall stand before kings...
—HOLY BIBLE, KING JAMES VERSION, PROVERBS 11:12

How to Materialize Your Desires

Desire rules men, the strong rule the weak.

—INSCRIPTION IN THE BRITISH MUSEUM

I n life, we are constantly battling with the problem of overcoming the hurdles that stand in the way of achieving our goals. Overcoming obstacles can be learned. Some people know it from birth. It requires self-discipline, training and practice.

Another of the most important factors responsible for human success or failure is self-image. Every person has two personalities: one as the world sees him/her and the other as he or she is in reality. A poor self-image can cause many complications in life and retard one's performance as a human being. Needless to say, a poor self-image affects all three levels of human existence—the physical, mental and spiritual.

Self-image takes a long time to form. Any inherited limitation—such as that endowed by the family of birth, the social set-up, the upbringing and the environment we live in—all greatly influence our thinking and our self-image. A doctor's son has little difficulty in trying to become a doctor. He might, however, have trouble trying to be a poet or a painter.

The simple reason is that where one lives places a limitation upon the person. If you are not happy about your environment, do something constructive about it. If the place where you live is not suitable for achieving your aims, it may well give you an inferiority complex. You can change your self-image by changing your residence, changing your country of residence, changing your profession, and changing your outlook on life by making friends with successful people. All this will have to be carefully planned.

It will take a long time to change your self-image from bad to good. But it can be done, in stages. First, try to handle small things right, so that you build up your self-confidence. And, as your self-confidence increases gradually with personal achievements, try bigger things so that one day you will have changed your entire self-image. It is hard but it can be done.

While your self-image is changing for the better, take precautions not to associate with negative people, who may not understand your process of personal development. They may discourage you. They may even resent your success and try to belittle you—to keep you back among the under-achievers like themselves. This period of transition (from a failure complex to a success-consciousness) is extremely delicate.

In fact, all outer influences of others (no matter how good or bad they be) should be avoided while working to achieve this goal.

Once this process has been completed, then comes the job of getting confident about it. From today, trust yourself a little more than you did yesterday, and cement this self-trust by succeeding in small projects first and then in bigger ones.

Your thinking pattern must be changed from a negative to a positive one. It will not be easy to do this, because a change in attitude requires a considerable degree of determination, persistence and patience. But it is very much worth the effort to invest in all three, and to improve yourself. You'll never do it if you don't ever start.

Thomas Edison was sent home from school because he was "too stupid to learn anything." He became the greatest inventor in history. You see—there is a very thin line between an idiot and a genius.

Consciously or unconsciously, when faced with a major problem, we tend to look at our own image and see whether we can handle it successfully or not. A bad self-image would lead to a negative attitude, negative actions and feelings, and pessimism about the outcome of a new project. Whatever we truly believe our capabilities are, our subconscious knows—and will bring about, in reality, results that exactly match our beliefs.

Remember, it is quite hard to change a bad habit, but it most certainly can be done.

The best way is to think positive thoughts and to feel positive by reading biographies of positive and successful people. It is also vital (during the process of change) to keep away from all negative people. One very great factor here is full faith in the efforts we make to bring about this change. We must understand that we can undo the negativity we find in our present way of thinking if we only work at it long enough. When we are more persistent than the problem, then we are, indeed, victorious.

In the transitional stages, when our poor self-image is changing to a better one, even a slight negative influence from a doubting friend can ruin our chances of success. Hence it is necessary to stay well clear of all negative influences until the self-image has been completely changed and firmly established. A newly-acquired better image can be easily destroyed, if we keep associating with negative, pessimistic, and failure-prone persons.

If you are really interested in yourself, find out what you really are. Take a real inventory, listing your assets and skills, as well as under-developed and poorer qualities, which need your attention. Then make plans to change your self-image to a better one, and hone the skills you do possess. Keep working at it till you succeed, and you shall be a totally new person. And as a man thinketh, so is he. You can think healthy thoughts and be crowned by success, health, harmony and happiness. It is up to you to take charge of your life and do your part. We wrongly believe that great people are very rare. The truth is, we all are great in our own ways. We just aren't all using our greatness, or living up to it.

There are certain facts or formulas of success and happiness that can be easily learned by anyone who has ordinary intelligence. The first thing is to accept yourself with all your faults and shortcomings. Then proceed to improve upon those failings, analyzing day-to-day actions to see where they need improvement, building better habits to replace what is not so great.

Mind you, nothing is ever achieved without personal efforts. If you want to write a book, be a politician, be a successful speaker, or even yearn to be a world leader, this can be achieved if you have a sincere desire and enough ambition to succeed and are willing to work, work, and go on working at it.

As the captain of your own ship, the navigator of your own life, you must steer yourself to realize your aims. And it is not as difficult as it may seem at first. To win and succeed in a project is largely a matter of habit and attitude. Try to overcome easy obstacles first and gain valuable experience and self-confidence. This will improve your self-image. Most of us can do much better than we think we can.

A person who never tries, neither succeeds nor fails. Of course, it is important to have faith in your own potential and the capacity to successfully achieve your goal. But it is a better idea to concentrate more on your positive qualities and successes of the past. Repeat them over to yourself, like the beads of a rosary. Enjoy that feeling of success you got, from doing them well. If you want more success and prosperity, you must first convince yourself that you really need them to the exclusion of everything else. Then you must proceed to focus in and earn them.

The problem with most of us is that for generations we have been taught wrong things by our parents, our friends, our churches and our society. We are meant to be healthy, happy and successful according to the Divine plan, but we have gone astray. Most things in nature are simple. It always helps to look for methods of solving a problem in an uncomplicated way.

Even the most experienced magician cannot fool the kids. Why? Just because kids look for simple explanations of the tricks performed and they spot the deception. When we become like children, most problems melt away and much success is achieved with the greatest ease.

You, too, can succeed in anything you desire. From the day you decide to achieve a specific goal, you will have to concentrate fully on that, all the time, and focus all your energies to realize it. That is the way to success. Almost anything can be done as long as we have a clear idea of what we desire and focus on achieving it. The most important thing is to persist until we succeed. A saint is a sinner who never gave up! To be realistic, however, we, as human beings have limitations as far as materializing our desires is concerned.

Bad Habits

Habits, which are largely responsible for our success or failure, have to be worked on; wrong ones that produce failure have to be analyzed and replaced by success-producing ones. Good habits make us, while bad ones can break us. And it takes a very strong will to change a bad habit to good. This process is not easy, because we find it easier and more pleasant to keep doing things the way we have always done them, even when our usual result is failure. Unconsciously, if we expect failure, we will get failure. Our bodies get so accustomed to moving in the old grooves that any thought of change creates discomfort. So, poor habits of thinking control our actions.

For example, if I am convinced that white bread tastes great and is good for me, even if a nutritionist points out to me that I should switch to whole wheat bread, I will listen to him and understand him intellectually, but may not be able or willing to act on his advice because the whole wheat bread has a different, unfamiliar taste. I am hooked on the taste of the white bread even though I know it is bad for me. The choice of right foods has a lot to do with your energy level.

Those who live to eat, rarely have a lot of stamina. To succeed in life, we must have right habits of living. Many saints have said as much. A lack of energy as a result of bad eating habits makes one lazy, without any zest for life. It can give rise to ill-health, restricted bodily movement, and cause many bodily aberrations very hard to diagnose and cure. A balanced way of living is ideal for achieving success. A bad physical condition will affect your thinking in a negative way, which will lead to a lack of self-confidence and induce doubt about your potentialities and possibilities.

Doubts and uncertainties about your success-potential totally block the energy release of the human body, and can make you feel half-dead despite being full of energy within. It is the release of energy that makes you function. If you have a million dollars in a bank, but your bank will not release your money, for whatever reason, you must behave like a poor man until your funds are available. It is not what we have, but what is available to us when needed, that counts. The consciousness of vitality is of prime importance. Our movements are dominated by our thoughts. The real battle lies in dealing with the quirks of our personalities. If you can temporarily remove all your inhibitions, and firmly believe that you can achieve great things, this temporary belief will release tremendous amounts of energy from within your system to perform great tasks, (but only as long as you continue to hold that belief without a doubt.)

The traditions of our society and our reactions to them have so set our physiological and psychological makeup that we don't know any better than what we are presented with. We think that we are helpless beings, totally at the mercy of politicians and leaders of organized religion, who make rules for our conduct in our daily lives. We, in our ignorance, behave like meek little children, without any hope of improved conditions or chance to elevate ourselves, when we could instead reclaim our birthright from our Creator as His children, made in His image, full of strength and the capability to create at will what we wish, as He does. But the fault lies with us. We have forgotten—hence, we suffer.

What May Limit Us: First, a Lack of Money

A lack of sufficient funds is a factor responsible for many of our failures. This can largely be the result of our wrong or inappropriate way of directing our thoughts. Since money is only a concept, it truly has no ultimate reality. But it is ingrained in our thoughts—"if I just had more money, I could do anything." This assumption is fallacious, inaccurate and illogical. It is also seriously limiting. Money, if correctly used, can indeed solve certain problems. If incorrectly used, it can create more problems than it can solve. It is only energy. How it is used determines whether it will do good or evil. Some high souls have done a lot of good with a limited amount of money, while others have done little with millions.

Schedule. Another limitation is placed upon us when we are in transit or in motion. The travel schedule can be so tight as to keep us all tied up, unable to attend to anything else. A business disorganization can make topsy-turvy conditions at home and at work. Breach of a business contract will impair our free and fair movement professionally.

Surroundings. Because of residential conditions, which might be inharmonious, you may not be free to do as you wish. This can cause all kinds of complications. Some people prefer to do most things at the office and keep their business interests away from home. Yet, if the circumstances at home be uncongenial, the person concerned will not accomplish much in either place and the result could be disastrous.

For all those who are too involved in their projects to worry about the "trivial problems at home," it would matter little whether the conditions at home were ideal or not. It is all a matter of personal preferences and choices. How we organize our priorities will largely determine whether we will be happy or miserable in a certain environment.

Relationships. A relationship places a great burden upon us in the form of responsibilities and obligations. Our children, too, may demand a lot of our attention, thus limiting our freedom of action. Their needs, now and in the future, for food, clothing, and education—can impinge on our own needs and freedoms. Financial investments require a lot of attention and may limit a person's capabilities, at times. All the invest-ments made unwisely can be a root cause of much anguish for the entire family, total failure of personal plans, and eventual poor health as a result of anxiety about future security. Financial misfortune in a game of chance may cause one to lose sight of his or her commitments. Even a love affair that goes well has a direct impact on all our dealings with others, and can totally divert our attention from business, perhaps at a critical moment.

Business and family ties. Some of our colleagues and subordinates can limit our freedom because of their misfortunes and problems, which may take many forms—an illness in the family, a financial quandary or a social obligation.

The circumstances surrounding our partners (in marriage or business) can restrict our freedom to a large extent. All those people we are bound up with by common interests of policy, love or hate, affect our conduct in life. For instance, joining a political party or belonging to a church of a particular denomination affects our actions or social behavior, according to the policies or beliefs of the church or the political party.

A marriage partner's financial resources, if depleted, can be the cause of our loss of freedom. Any money borrowed from any source can take away our power of thinking and doing things freely. When our parents speculate, any losses incurred may create very nasty situations, thus hampering our freedom.

The nefarious activities of in-laws or even of distant relatives can pose a substantial threat to our own families, our financial future and well-being. Sometimes a lengthy legal tangle can be very costly socially (in the form of loss of valuable contacts, if nothing worse) as well as financially. Overseas investments, relationships (personal or business), and all commitments become areas of great concern, should the economic or political situation in that country suddenly become unpredictable and uncertain, as in the case of Hong Kong when it became independent of British rule.

Your personal reputation may receive a reverse blow or your business environment may most unexpectedly become uncongenial as a result of some outsider's influence, thus limiting your freedom of thought and action. At such times, your home atmosphere may be totally dictated by people beyond your control.

A platonic relationship, a highly ambitious undertaking involving huge masses of people, and those aspirations whose success depends upon the whims of others, can be reasons for our loss of maneuverability in business.

Factors That Support Success

We have been discussing how various kinds of limitations may adversely affect our performance; but now we shall focus our attention on factors that support our success-producing efforts.

An ingredient vital to success is *encouragement*. Without this, our entire system is paralyzed and no energy is released to do even the small things we consider trivial. We all need encouragement. Each of us should focus on the positive qualitiesof people as we perceive them, and encourage one another by making positive statements.

Point out good traits, ignore the negative ones, and state the stronger ones more than once so that they register on the mind of the other person. All great feats are performed through inspiration. *We can do it together.*

Create Your Own Orbit of Positive Friends

If you don't yet have friends who are positive, create them by praying to God sincerely and repeatedly till He answers. Things will start to shape up, new avenues will open and you will find yourself in circumstances that never existed before. You will have new opportunities to make new friends. Caution: Don't try to judge all those you meet; keep an open mind and be receptive and broad-minded.

Take the hint that the Almighty Creator has responded to your prayers. Don't waste your opportunities by using your limited logic to try to analyze everything. God knows best. Give His love to all and your scope of friends will increase a thousandfold. This approach will attract friends and they will help you realize your dreams, provided you give them your love unconditionally, expecting nothing in return. Don't try to make deals with God. We are not meant to carry the burden of our lives all by ourselves. Make sure you create your own orbit of positive friends.

Avoid people who are negative because they sap our energies, which are meant to be used for useful pursuits and for the benefit of humanity. Successful people have many friends to help them succeed. Remember, no one can succeed in any project all alone without any help from others. Some have three friends, while others have thirty, and the saints have hundreds. The more friends we have, the easier it is to carry the burden of life. They inspire us and encourage us to do great things.

True friends point out our faults, help us by giving solid and practical advice, and provide moral support by giving us love. They make us aware of our limitations by evaluating our potentialities and real wants, accurately, truthfully.

The qualities of a real friend are: Honesty, sympathy in the hour of grief and need, and willingness to help in crises. A true friend will watch out for your benefit. He will be generous to a fault and sympathetic in case of adversity. In need, you can count on him. A friendship has to be unselfish or it will not last.

The greatest gift of God to man is a true friend and there is no other relationship, I repeat no other, that is more valuable than to have a true friend. It has to be unconditional. Selfish relations are temporary and do not stand the tests of time. God speaks through the mouth of a true friend. But true friendship has to be nursed and cherished on both ends. It is the best investment you can make, and will pay dividends a thousandfold. The wise know this fact and value friendship accordingly.

Questions and Answers

Q. What is the difference between a desire and a wish?

A: The main difference between a desire and a wish is how much willpower backs up the wanting. A wish, when backed up by the force of will, becomes a desire. Merely wishing for something never achieves anything. "If wishes were horses, beggars would ride."

Q: What are the likely stumbling blocks in our bid to materialize our desires?

A: Generally speaking, there are many factors that can cause a delay or utter failure in materializing our desires, like self-doubt, which means we do not trust what we can do. This lack of self-confidence does not allow the body to release the energies required to succeed.

A desire has to be materialized on its plane of birth. Success on the material plane requires money, physical and mental energy, the expertise and help of others in form of practical suggestions, input, financial collaboration and a winning attitude. When we can avail ourselves of all these, then material success can be assured. When these are not available to us, each can be a stumbling block.

Q: *What transforms a desire into reality?*

A: When the entire being backs up a desire on all the levels of existence, then it materializes on the physical plane. Any kind of internal conflict may block all progress. Suppose I want to buy a Lincoln or a Cadillac, but am not sure that in my circumstances I am justified in spending the money for such an expensive car. My own uncertainty can cause a mental conflict. A part of me may not agree with my desire for an expensive car; it may have a different set of uses for that money, which it feels are more important. Such a conflict of moral values can be ruinous on a higher plane and any investment of time, money, physical and mental energies on something you feel conflicted about, will be wasted.

Before you let yourself really desire something, be sure that you don't suffer from any conflicts within. You have to have the cooperation of your heart and soul. One more thing. You must desire something to the exclusion of everything else. This means it should be the thing you desire most. Such a cooperation of body, mind and soul transforms a burning desire into a reality.

We "will" it to materialize. And it must, because we all can create things through our will. The transformation is a gradual process and takes place in stages. Our faith in our ability to create at will, and unshakable confidence in the future outcome of our efforts, are the two major factors that boost the creative process enormously. No matter how difficult our external circumstances may appear, our mental environment must stay congenial and calm. This sort of quiet confidence and faith is a sure sign that real progress is being made and success in our project is on the horizon.

Q: *What is visualization and how does it work?*

A: There are two aspects of visualization: One is the theory and the other is the practice. What works theoretically may not work practically. If a theory is based on fallacious assumptions, it will never stand the practical tests. Most books I have read do not give precise instructions on this subject. The key points are missing. Mere imagination of success, no matter how tempting the pictures, never materializes a desire. It is *the living in it* that does. Living in it involves you on the physical, mental and spiritual planes. In the physical, all five senses must be involved. To all intents and purposes, if all the above is not included, visualization will remain an exercise in futility.

This process is a definite technique that requires concentration of mind, accompanied by full control of the senses. The key here is the emotional attachment to the materialization of a desire. If such a materialization does not touch the person's emotions, then this discrepancy will manifest as a failure of the visualization technique.

To motivate its salesmen, a company published pictures of top sellers with the expensive cars they had won in sales contests, and told trainees "Imagine yourself in that picture." Very few could do that.

But when they said: "Imagine yourself driving that wonderful new car down your home street. Imagine your hands on the steering wheel, smell the rich new-car smell, feel the buttery leather of the seat beneath you, hear the glorious sounds of your favorite music on the stereo—taste the success you have won as you pull up in front of your house and your family compliments you on the great new car you have won!" Many more prize winners resulted, and both the company and its salesmen enjoyed great success.

To that refined image of success, add heart—and soon you too will be enjoying that kind of tangible success.

> *There are two tragedies in life.*
> *One is not to get your heart's desire.*
> *The other is to get it.*
>
> —GEORGE BERNARD SHAW

Believe You Can Succeed— and You Will

*One person with a belief is equal to a force of
ninety-nine who have only interests.*

—JOHN STUART MILL

In the previous chapters we have discussed:
- How to build a great new future
- Man's unlimited potential
- Creating a foundation
- Opportunities and Timing—Keys to success
- Yoga of action
- How people who surround you can make or break you
- The star guide for businessmen
- Focusing your energies for success
- How to materialize your desires

This chapter principally deals with your beliefs and successes, laying special emphasis on applying the techniques we have learned so far. Now that we have completed our homework, let us put everything together.

To succeed in a project, you first decide on what you want to achieve. Then, like building a house, you have to decide on a location. After that the plans have to be drawn up. The next step will be the foundation. Construction of a house requires getting all the materials together. Once all this is done, you proceed with the actual construction with the help of skilled workers.

In your chosen project a similar procedure has to be followed:
- Know your project

- Decide on your time frame
- Determine the geographical location
- Establish a budget
- Decide on a blueprint
- Locate manpower (experts and expertise)
- Set target date for various stages of completion
- Put ingredients together
- Add creativity, persistence, hard work and optimism

Thus far, all looks good. It is imperative at this juncture to create an overall plan of action and pursue each step systematically till the entire project is completed to your satisfaction. Flowcharts really do prevent disasters!

I have observed that many people, going ahead with a project involving their life's savings and the future of their entire family, will still fail to consider these important factors:

- Ages of all the people involved
- Their financial status
- Right or wrong geographical location
- Timing from the personal point of view
- What repercussions the project will have on all the individuals concerned. The only motivating force they possess is the desire for "success"—which they could neither describe nor recognize.

The greater the stakes in life, the greater is the penalty of failure. This penalty can take many forms. It can lead to total financial ruin, depleted health or disease if the place is wrong (non-salubrious) for your health or others, and total uncertainty of the future of all the people involved.

There has to be a method or technique of succeeding in a project and proceeding properly with it, planned right from its infancy. A farmer does not go ahead at random and sow corn at any time, in any type of soil, in any weather, with a total disregard for the phase of the moon, with only one desire: To produce a nice corn crop.

In order for us to be successful in reaching our goals, all obstacles must be overcome. Either we succeed in overcoming the obstacles, or we are overcome by them. Some obstacles may be wrong timing, lack of opportunities, absence of people who harmonize with and support us, a wrong location, or a lack of resources, financial or otherwise. A lack of wisdom and forethought is particularly critical.

As shown in the success formula, the most conducive environment for success is produced by living in a location favorable for our material success (which can be determined through astrology) and, if we start our project in a propitious time, with adequate resources at our disposal, success is sure to follow. In order to reach our goals, we must associate with positive people who are sympathetic to our aims, while avoiding those who would stand in our way. Not only do we need to associate with positive and harmonious people, but also we must be persistent ourselves, work hard and keep a positive mental attitude.

We must navigate our ship of life by carefully steering clear of insurmountable obstacles, some of which, like an iceberg, may be only partially visible. The Titanic, the most powerful ship ever built, despite warnings, went full steam ahead and collided with an iceberg, meeting with total disaster, including the loss of many lives and the sinking of the ship. Obstacles too large or too treacherous, that cannot be surmounted, must be circumvented through skillful navigation. You don't want to sail into any icebergs. At times, people whose intentions are treacherous can hold us back or make us fail in our plans: We must steer clear of people who would try to put obstacles in our way or torpedo our projects.

In order for a house to stand firm, it must be built on a solid foundation. The pillars that support the structure of our lives are: faith in ourselves, faith in a higher Intelligence or God, hope, hard work and anticipation of ultimate success.

There is a saying: "In order to be successful, we must be at the right place at the right time." We all know that success in business depends on location, location, and location. Right geographical location is one of the big secrets of life. There are different places where we feel healthy, others where we are more successful in making money, yet others are favorable for romance and relationships. Some locations are favorable for spiritual evolution. Some people move to a certain location after analyzing economic, climatic and cultural factors. Others are intuitively drawn to locations where they feel they can become successful in their cherished aims, be they material, artistic, mental or spiritual.

However, it can be determined accurately through astrology just which country and city will be most conducive to your health, money, love and spiritual evolution, even though you may not find them all at the same geographical location.

Making preparations for moving ahead to attain our goals is much like getting ready to climb a high mountain. We have to have mental and bodily discipline in place so we can be in control, determine the direction we are going to take, analyze our assets, plan our course ahead, create a step-by-step blueprint, concentrate, visualize the successful outcome of our project, expect positive results, and above all, never lose our balance of mind.

When preparing to climb a high mountain, we must be aware of the risks involved, and know whether we have the physical stamina, willpower, as well as resources (time, money and support) required to carry out our plans. We must determine which stage of development we will be at when we embark on a project, and when we finish. We must review our priorities and other commitments that could distract our attention and concentration at that stage.

Successful completion of a project requires a tremendous degree of energy. Our energy is highest from the age of twenty-one until fifty, when it starts to decline. During the high-energy phase, you are in great shape because you have the advantage of having a high I.Q., maximum energy, enthusiasm and an adventurous spirit. Starting a project during this state increases the chances of your success in any project to about 90 percent.

When you are between the age of fifty and seventy, you will benefit from your experience of life, knowledge, sobriety of mind and greater contacts, but your energy will be diminished. During the low energy phase after seventy, your energy will be least. But you will have maturity of mind, resources and increased contacts, which will be your greatest allies.

It is not only important to have plenty of physical and mental energy, but we must also focus all our energies on one goal at a time. Sunrays focused through a magnifying glass can light a fire.

Scattered energies lead to meager results, but focused concentration can virtually burn away any obstacle.

The human body and mind operate like energy reservoirs. The human brain possesses billions of watts of energy. It is without limitation, if we only knew how properly to access and use it. Our body contains various energies, physical, mental and spiritual, which are released at different times, according to our needs and the demands made on them. Our body is like a reservoir that has a great capacity to store large amounts of energies. To store them, we must concentrate mentally and fill our inner reservoirs. When a demand is made on any of these energies, that type of energy is automatically released.

Once a woman's son was trapped under a car and in danger of being crushed. In her anguish, she made a frantic demand on herself and was able to lift the car long enough for her son to be pulled to safety. This appears to be a miracle, but it is a fact. The amounts of energy released will depend upon the reservoir's capacity and the degree of concentration exercised. Athletes are able to tap great amounts very suddenly by making a demand in an emergency or even at a time when they think they cannot go on any longer. Most of us go through life without realizing how much energy and which type we have in store. We are ignorant of our capabilities and potentialities.

Energy Is Life

There is no limit to your potential; use your willpower and concentration to make a demand from your system and the energy required will be released to successfully attain whatever goal you have set your heart and mind upon. Do not doubt it.

"The success of all great men and women has been generated by the obstacles they overcame. The greater the obstacles, the greater their success," says M.R. Kopmeyer in *How You Can Get Richer Quicker.*

The technique of visualization has many aspects: Hope, strong desire, expectation and self-confidence—and, last but not least, your strong belief in yourself and your future.

If you think you are beaten you are.
If you think you dare not, you don't.
It's all in the state of mind.
But sooner or later, the man who wins
Is the fellow who thinks he can.

—ANONYMOUS

Don't depend on someone else to materialize your dream. Make your own dreams come true by depending upon yourself. Self-dependence saves time, money and energy. It gets things done. If you can control your thoughts, you can dominate your circumstances. Lack of faith in yourself reduces your chances of success in a project. Don't doubt. Be confident. Don't set limits. Be open and magnanimous in your thinking. Expand your consciousness. And always keep on doing your best.

Most people's life can be summed up in a few words. For example, a man finds a physically good-looking woman. If he is an Aries, he will fall in love with her haircut, being totally blinded by the exterior. They will marry on an impulse, buy a house and a car on a mortgage, have a few children and make money. They will prepare for retirement with an IRA. Just after retirement, they will take a trip to a pilgrimage place because they fear fast-approaching death, to make a compromise with God—after having ignored Him during their heyday. Finally they die in harness.

What about the mental and spiritual development that should occur in a lifetime? We cannot afford to ignore those facets of human life. We have to focus on the development of the total person. Our hurry-up materialistic culture teaches us to want everything without effort or sacrifice (physical or mental), which won't happen because it would be a violation of the natural law. If I want to get to heaven, I have to die. There is no other way. We lead two lives: one internal, the other external. The real treasure of a person lies within, but we Westerners make the mistake of ignoring it. What a pity.

This book was written to give you practical techniques to get through life more easily, being armed with the suggestions given. The formulas or formulae given here are not hypothetical. They are techniques that have worked before and will work for you, if you work with them sincerely.

Do not expect to change your life overnight! It takes time, effort and patience to make a better future. Rome was not built in a day. You should be skeptical of all those who offer a quick fix and promise to solve your problems miraculously. Bear in mind that miracles are not brought about in contradiction to the natural laws. The Architect of the universe chooses not to violate His or Her own laws; we also should not violate them. We are given a free will so that we may realize our mistakes, change our ways and improve our lot, and thus be victorious over our obstacles.

You possess a great source of power that flows through you from God, and you will be wise to claim your birthright by taking charge of your life and not just sitting about aimlessly, pitying yourself. My friend, life is a battle and the weaklings (those who are mentally too lazy to act and want to blame everyone else for their misery) are run over by the strong and left behind.

Be a warrior, take every problem as a challenge, and focus all your energies (physical, mental and spiritual) to overcome it. Act we must, willingly or unwillingly. And that is the law. I mean the law of nature. There is no way a soul can get out of the bodily bondage without performing action. I hope you will choose to act wisely and proceed toward a path of self-perfection as many saints have done. We can all learn a great deal from their examples. May the forces of good be with you, and may you never be the same again!

Questions and Answers

Q: Why is my positive belief required in order to succeed?

A: It is hard to think of a situation where a person could accomplish even small things without a certain degree of belief in himself or herself. Beliefs and hopes for the future give us impetus to keep moving forward. The firmer the belief, the harder we try to succeed, and that is what largely contributes to faith, and to our final successes.

Q: How do faith and belief work?

A: These go hand in hand. We can't have one without the other. They form the cornerstones of our life's foundation. No hopes survive without both. Faith and belief in self and others are abstract things so vital to human existence, but we can't see them. They strengthen our mental health by giving it more fixity of purpose and justification of our actions, which adds to our strength of purpose. Doubts of self and others sap our energy but, properly guided, "faith can move mountains" as the Bible says.

Our intentions have to be honorable for best results. Even if the intent be dishonorable, faith will still get the desired results, but the laws of nature will be violated (if lies were told and people were cheated out of money) because dishonorable things hurt other people. We can't afford to achieve our aims at the cost of other people's interests which is why win/win solutions to difficulties or disagreements are always best.

Q: I am a pleasure seeker. I like to have fun. Is there any hope for me?

A: Yes, there is hope for everyone. Are you sure you have had enough fun? If you are like a bug in a rug, you will not stop having fun.

Only when you are bored with "fun" and your senses are tired and you would like pleasure on a different level—meaning after the physical pleasures come mental and spiritual pleasure, which are superior to the physical, but you, blinded by the physical, do not yet perceive this.

In fact, in the spiritual realm a yogi reaches a state of bliss which is the highest form of joy a person can achieve on Earth.

It is important to know whether or not you still desire more fun. If yes, then I cannot help you. You must help yourself.

If you now desire a different type of fun than the physical, what is your preference; intellectual recreation or spiritual evolution?

If the answer is the latter, congratulations! You are now ready to steer your ship in the spiritual waters and study the practice of Yoga that will eventually take you to your spiritual goal.

Q: A lot of what you say seems to be based on Astrology. What if I don't believe in all of that crap? Can I still benefit from your book?

A: Yes, certain statements I have made were based on astrology (both tropical and sidereal). You don't have to believe in it but it certainly is no crap. Over many centuries, all the people who wielded power have sought astrological counsel to help guide their actions.

Napoleon consulted Pierre le Clerc, King Edward VII consulted The Great Cheiro, Queen Elizabeth I worked with John Dee, Field Marshal Lord Kitchener with Cheiro, Madame Blavatsky was guided by Alan Leo, J.P. Morgan weighed both financial and personal moves with Evangeline Adams, and there are many more such instances I could cite. They can't all be wrong.

If you are not open to suggestions, it will be hard for you to learn new things.

Life is a matter of attitude. With a positive mental attitude and a little willingness to listen, you will find that many wise people will be willing to help you.

Whether you believe in astrology or not, you can still benefit from this book because it contains proven formulas for achieving true and lasting success, which are all squarely based on the natural laws. "All things are possible for the one who believeth."

Without a belief a man is
helpless against the dragons.

—HEYWOOD BROUN

Index

Bibliography

Battista, O.A. *People Power.* Fort Worth, Texas: Research Services Corporation, 1977.

Berg, Karen, and Andrew Gilman, with Edward P. Stevenson. *Get To the Point.* New York: Bantam Books, 1989.

Bliss, Edwin C. *Getting Things Done.* New York: Bantam Books, 1976.

Bristol, Claude M. *The Magic of Believing.* Englewood Cliffs, New Jersey: Prentice Hall, 1959.

Chopra, Deepak, M.D. *Ageless Body, Timeless Mind.* New York, Harmony Books, 1993.

Conklin, Robert. *How to Get People to Do Things.* New York: Ballantine Books, 1979.

Covey, Stephen R. *The 7 Habits of Highly Effective People.* New York, Simon & Schuster, 1989.

Hill, Napoleon. *Think and Grow Rich.* New York: Hawthorne Books, Inc., 1937.

Hill, Napoleon and Clement W. Stone. *SuccessThrough a Positive Mental Attitude,* Englewood Cliffs, New Jersey: Prentice Hall, 1960.

Huxley, Aldous. *The Perennial Philosophy.* London: Fontana Books, 1946.

Kopmeyer, M.R. *How You Can Get Richer....Quicker!* Louisville, Kentucky: M.R. Kopmeyer, 1975.

Lakein, Alan. *How to Get Control of Your Time and Your Life.* New York: David McKay Co. Inc., 1973.

LeBoeuf, Michael, Ph.D. *Working Smart.* New York, Warner Books, 1979.

Losovy, Lewis E. *Turning People On*. Englewood Cliffs, New Jersey, Prentice Hall, 1977.

Mahoney, Michael J. *Self-Change: Strategies for Solving Personal Problems*. New York: W.W. Norton & Company, 1979.

Maltz, Maxwell, M.D. "A New Technique for Using Your Subconscious Power." In *Psycho-Cybernetics*. Englewood Cliffs, New Jersey: Prentice Hall, 1960.

Mangan, James T. *The Secret of Perfect Living*. Englewood Cliffs, New Jersey: Prentice Hall, 1963.

Murphy, Joseph, DRS., D.D. Ph.D. LL.D., *The Amazing Laws of Cosmic Mind Power*. West Nyack, New York: Parking Publishing, 1965.

Murphy, Joseph, DRS., D.D. Ph.D. LL.D., *The Power of Your Subconscious Mind*. Englewood Cliffs, New Jersey: Prentice Hall, 1965.

Newman, Mildred and Bernard Berkowitz, with Jean Owen. *How to be Your Own Best Friend*. New York: Ballantine Books, 1971.

Olson, Robert W. *The Art of Creative Thinking. A Practical Guide*. New York: Harper & Row Publishers, 1978.

Peale, Norman Vincent. *The Power of Positive Thinking*. New York, Fawcett Columbine, 1953.

Peale, Norman Vincent. *Enthusiasm Makes the Difference*. New York: Fawcett Columbine, 1967.

Peale, Norman Vincent. *You Can If You Think You Can*. Englewood Cliffs, New Jersey: Prentice Hall, 1974.

Ponder, Catherine. *The Prosperity Secret of the Ages*. Englewood Cliffs, New Jersey: Prentice Hall, 1964.

Schwartz, David J. *The Magic of Thinking Big*. Englewood Cliffs, New Jersey, Prentice Hall, 1959.

*Seabury, David. *Stop Being Afraid*. Los Angeles: Science of Mind Publications 1965.

Sher, Barbara, with Annie Gottlieb. *Wishcraft. How to Get What You Really Want*. New York: Viking, 1974.

Yogananda, Paramahansa. *Autobiography of a Yogi*. Los Angeles: Self-Realization Fellowship, 1946.

Yoganada, Paramahansa. *The Divine Romance.* Collected talks and
essays. Vols. i & ii,Los Angeles: Self-Realization
Fellowship, 1986

Yoganada, Paramahansa. *Man's Eternal Quest.* Los Angeles: Self-
Realization Fellowship, 1975.

Yoganada, Paramahansa. *The Science of Religion.* Los Angeles:
Self-Realization Fellowship, 1953.

Yoganada, Paramahansa. *Where There Is Light. A practical hand-
book.* Los Angeles: Self-Realization Fellowship, 1988.

Yoganada, Paramahansa. *Scientific Healing Affirmations.* Los
Angeles: Self-Realization Fellowship, 1958.

Yoganada, Paramahansa. *Whispers From Eternity.* Los Angeles:
Self-Realization Fellowship, 1935.

*Indicates out-of-print title.

The Author-Ostaro

About the Author

Ostaro believes in helping people help themselves. His philosophy is Eastern, his approach to problem-solving is Western—two factors which contribute heavily to the depth of his insight into human nature. He firmly believes that positive thinking leads to positive results.

He was born in a Vedic family in Delhi, India. He lived in England for several years where he pursued a career in journalism. While in Paris, he researched the Caballah, as well as astrology. He came to the United States in 1973.

He is world-renowned as a Hindu astrologer who is right. He correctly foretold the breakup of the Soviet Union, the five winners of the 1986 World Series in baseball, both of Bill Clinton's presidential races, plus the New York elections of Governor George Pataki, and most recently, Senator Hillary Clinton.

Ostaro produces and hosts, *Think Big,* a talk show on Channel 57 (Time Warner Cable TV; New York City). He is a motivational speaker and a Toastmaster. He has been featured in *The New York Times, The Wall Street Journal, The Daily News,* and *The New Yorker.* He has been a guest on several radio and television shows. He is a member of the Screen Actors Guild and The American Federation of Television and Radio Artists. He was cast as a swami in the Woody Allen movie, *Stardust Memories.*

In 1979, Ostaro founded Inter-National Development, Improvement and Assistance, (I.N.D.I.A.) Inc., a non-profit organization dedicated to positive thinking, self-help and psychical research in New York

The Art and Craft of Success: 10 Steps
Order Form

FAX ORDERS:
   Fax this form to: (646) 424-9130
TELEPHONE ORDERS:
   Please call: (212) 686-4121
POSTAL ORDERS:
   Svarg Syndicate, Inc. • P.O. Box 20340• Greely Sq. Station
   New York, NY 10001 • USA • Telephone (212) 686-4121

Please send *The Art and Craft of Success: 10 Steps*
$15.00 plus shipping

Number of copies: _____

Name: _____

Company: _____

Address: _____

City: _____ State: _____ Zip: _____

E-mail address: _____

SHIPPING:
   • US: $4.00 for the first book and $2.00 for each additional copy.
   • INTERNATIONAL: $9.00 for the first book and $6.00 for each
   additional copy.

PAYMENT:

_____ Check enclosed (Make your check payable to: Svarg Syndicate, Inc.)

_____ Visa _____ Master Card _____ AMEX _____ Discover

Card number: _____ Expiration date: _____

Signature: _____

Total enclosed: $ _____.

*I understand that I may return it at any time for a full refund—for
any reason, no questions asked.*

The Art and Craft of Success: 10 Steps
Order Form

FAX ORDERS:
Fax this form to: (646) 424-9130

TELEPHONE ORDERS:
Please call: (212) 686-4121

POSTAL ORDERS:
Svarg Syndicate, Inc. • P.O. Box 20340• Greely Sq. Station
New York, NY 10001 • USA • Telephone (212) 686-4121

Please send *The Art and Craft of Success: 10 Steps*
$15.00 plus shipping

Number of copies: _____

Name: _____

Company: _____

Address: _____

City: _____ State: _____ Zip: _____

E-mail address: _____

SHIPPING:
• US: $4.00 for the first book and $2.00 for each additional copy.
• INTERNATIONAL: $9.00 for the first book and $6.00 for each additional copy.

PAYMENT:

_____ Check enclosed (Make your check payable to: Svarg Syndicate, Inc.)

_____ Visa _____ Master Card _____ AMEX _____ Discover

Card number: _____ Expiration date: _____

Signature: _____

Total enclosed: $ _____.

I understand that I may return it at any time for a full refund—for any reason, no questions asked.